WHEN THE
BOUGH
BREAKS

WORLD WAR II—MEMORIES OF
OPERATION PIED PIPER

JOAN KELLEHER

Excerpts from Winnie-the-Pooh by A.A. Milne, published 1926

WHEN THE BOUGH BREAKS
World War II—Memories of Operation Pied Piper

Battersea Origins Press
ISBN: 978-1-7369597-0-1 (print)
ISBN: 978-1-7369597-1-8 (eBook)

For my children:
Christopher, Lisa, Dennery, Kaleo and John

ROCK-A-BYE BABY

Rock-a-bye baby, on the treetops,
When the wind blows, the cradle will rock,
When the bough breaks, the cradle will fall,
And down will come baby, cradle and all.

Nursery Rhyme. The first printed version from *Mother Goose's Melody* (London, c. 1765)

CONTENTS

PREFACE

"Operation Pied Piper," code name for the evacuation of children from industrialized cities during World War II, begins four-year-old Joan's exile from London into the hands of foster families. For five years she survives the horrors of war and the hostilities of resentful foster parents by dreams of a perfect family waiting for her in a world at peace.

Evacuations started in September, 1939 and included school students with their teachers, mothers with their children, the elderly and other vulnerable adults. Over three million people were moved within the first four days. Upon arrival the children were lined up and chosen by a foster family. If you had a bed, you took in a child, whether you wanted to or not. You did get a government allowance for each child and their ration books.

This first-person account is a part of World War 11 history that many people are unaware of. Yet, there are children today who are still surviving the effects of war, of terrorism, of separation. This is their story too.

CHAPTER 1

EXODUS

The old grey donkey, Eeyore stood by himself in a thistly corner of the Forest, his front feet well apart, his head on one side, and thought about things. Sometimes he thought sadly to himself, "Why?" and sometimes he thought, "Wherefore?" and sometimes he thought, "Inasmuch as which?" and sometimes he didn't quite know what he was thinking about. A.A. Milne

London, September 1939

Soldiers with guns and bags and loud voices stand on the platform where we wait for our train – Mummy, Patsy, Johnny and me. Train tracks crisscross, black and shiny, over grey gravel as far as I can see. Trains rush past: a long blur of colour and noise; whoosh, and they are gone, pulling my hair, my coat with them. I hold Patsy's hand tight, and my one-legged teddy bear, Ted, tighter.

"The next train on platform eleven is going to…stopping at…" a lady's voice crackles and echoes around my head and a round-faced, black train chugs slowly up to our platform, sighing, screeching, metal on metal. Its smoke stings my eyes, its clanking bangs in my ears. I turn away, hide behind my mother's coat. It stops in front of us.

Soldiers climb onto the train. They all wear brown clothes and silly hats that won't keep the wind out of their ears or the sun out of their eyes. The train steps are high, and a gap, deep and black, separates the platform from the train. Patsy grabs my hand and pulls me over the hole, up the steep steps into a carriage filled with more soldiers. Shiny boots and prickly brown trousers crush me as if I'm not there at all. I put Ted under my arm and grab my mother's skirt, tight. She is carrying Johnny and I can't find her hand. A whistle blows, a man waves a green flag, yells "All clear," and slams the train doors shut with a bang that echoes, bang, bang, bang.

My stomach hurts.

Soldiers stand in front of seats filled with other soldiers. "'Ere, missus," the one with the red face says and puts our suitcases on the net rack and offers Mummy his seat. Mummy smiles as she sits and I scoot back on the prickly seat, squeezed between my mother and Patsy. Johnny wriggles on Mummy's lap, kicking my legs with his chubby feet wrapped in their white socks and tiny black shoes. Our train shakes forward, slowly, like old Mr. Cooper who stumbles along our street with his walking stick and scruffy old, skinny old, dog.

★ ★ ★

We had all sat together for tea that day – my brother Johnny in his high chair, sister Patsy, my mother and father. It was so quiet. No one spoke. The radio was off, no music at all and we always had music at teatime, the only sound was the tick of the clock on the mantelpiece and the clatter of cups placed on saucers. Even Johnny was quiet for a change; he didn't even bang his spoon, not once. It felt like something bad was about to happen, so, putting Ted under my arm, I decided to do something about the quiet.

Grabbing the back of my chair and climbing onto the big, fat cushion that boosted me up to the table I sang, as loud as I could, Mummy's favourite song, just like I had the other day. It had made her smile then. "Daisy, Daisy, give me your answer do/ I'm half-crazy all for the love…"

My father laughed and didn't try to hide it, and I told him I'm not going to sing any more, not ever.

"Get down, you'll fall," Mummy said. "You can help me if you like, I've lots to do."

"Well, I'll be going then, Maud," my father said and gave Mummy a kiss on her cheek.

"Cheerio, Pat," she said. And off he went.

I followed her into her bedroom, where I'm not usually allowed. It smelled like the roses in our garden and the powder Mummy dusted me with after my bath. She started packing suitcases, four of them, sitting open on the bed. I stood still, watching and listening as she sorted clothes, then spoke to herself: "Too small, not much wear left in that, this will do." I held Ted in front of me so he could see and waited.

"There, that's that," Mummy said as she buckled wide yellow straps around each of the four brown suitcases.

"Are we going on holiday, Mummy?"

"We're going away for a while, on a train. It won't be for long," she said as she walked out of the room.

I hurried after her, out of the empty room, and whispered in Ted's ear, "Don't worry Ted, we're going on a train. You'll like trains."

Patsy's big – seven years older than me and went to school and ignored me most of the time. But that day, Patsy helped me dress for our train ride.

"Brighton's a seaside town. It will be fun there," Patsy said. Why would we go to the seaside if it weren't a holiday?

Mummy brought the vase of roses from the living room to the kitchen, washed the vase until it sparkled and scrunched up the beautiful red flowers in newspaper for the dustman to pick up with the rubbish. I heard the snap as she bent them in half. She wrapped the roses so tight their velvet petals fell to the floor. I picked one up and rubbed it, smooth and soft, between my fingers and wondered why the roses could not come with us.

Sandwiches were made for the journey, mashed banana for me, with sugar on top – my favourite. Patsy put them in the basket on Johnny's pram, and Johnny and the luggage were packed in tight for the long walk to the station.

"Well, we're off," said Mother. She turned the key in the lock, pulled on the front door handle to make sure it was closed, and the letterbox flapped tick, tick.

Mummy had told us we could take one toy each. Patsy had packed her beautiful china doll in her suitcase; I wasn't allowed to touch her. Of course, I had Ted, though he's my friend. We were together all the time. Johnny kicked up a fuss when Mother gave him his long-eared, stuffed dog; he wanted his train and blocks and screamed all the way to the railroad station.

★ ★ ★

After a while, I peeked around the carriage and when the soldiers moved, I saw flashes of green and huge trees fly by outside the windows. We stopped at every station and more soldiers crowded on to the train. They talked and laughed loudly and smoked cigarettes and stepped on them with their boots. They swayed over me like they might fall and squash me flat. I didn't want my sandwich.

The train jerked to another shuddery stop. Patsy grabbed my hand and pulled me towards the door and down the steep steps. Soldiers put our suitcases on the platform, Johnny's pram appeared, and off we went. The wind blew hard in my face, making me push through it with every step. I clung to my mother's flapping skirt as I trotted along. We walked until my legs went wobbly. Mother said, "Here we are," opened the black iron gate in front of a large house and rang the lion-faced doorbell.

A stranger opened the door. She was fat and smiley and said her name was Mrs. Jupp, or maybe she said Mrs. Jubb, and she was pleased to have us, and Mummy could use her oven any day and not to worry about the sheets or towels, that she would boil them in the copper with her own every Monday. They talked together for a long time, Mummy and Mrs. Jupp, who then picked up two cases and carried them up the stairs. Patsy grabbed the other two and bumped them up the stairs, making as much noise as she could. As she moved away, I saw flowery carpets that brightened the hall and dark wooden doors that opened to sunny rooms.

Holding tight to the thick, carved banisters, I followed my mother as she carried Johnny up to the room we were given all to ourselves at the top of the house, in a seaside town called Brighton. Jewelled beams of light shimmered down in front of me as I climbed up the steep wooden staircase. My eyes followed those shafts of rainbow to a beautiful coloured glass window on a landing halfway up the large staircase. I wanted to stand in that rainbow forever – me and Mummy and Ted.

CHAPTER 2

BRIGHTON

Piglet sidled up to Pooh from behind. "Pooh," he whispered.
"Yes, Piglet?"
"Nothing," said Piglet, taking Pooh's paw. "I just wanted to be
sure of you." A.A. Milne

Our room was big and had windows on two sides, drawing in sunshine and light, which met in the middle, like a light bulb under a shade. Dark wooden floors smelled of polish, and two steps divided the room in half, like the landing in our house. (Ted and I had bumped down those for fun.) Except for a small blue rug in front of the gas fire, there were no carpets, and the room was bare except for a dresser, a square wooden table, four wooden chairs with spindly backs, two beds and a little cupboard with a hotplate on top.

"Home sweet home," Mummy said, and sighed. I looked for big, fat chairs, lace doilies, silk cushions…roses. It didn't look like home.

"Be careful, now," Mummy warned Johnny and me, pointing to the steps. "You must be quiet, no jumping, we don't want to disturb Mrs. Jupp." That was the smiley person who opened the door. Mummy called her Mrs. Jupp, but she told me I could call her Aunty.

Patsy turned away and made those tutting sounds, like when she doesn't want to eat her cabbage.

"We're evacuees," Mummy said, looking at Patsy, "and we don't want to cause any trouble. We're very lucky Mrs. Jupp let us stay."

I tugged Patsy's skirt, "What's an evacuee?"

"It means we have to leave London because of the stupid war."

"Is Daddy an evacuee?"

"Daddy's joined the army, he volunteered," Patsy whispered. "Shush. Mummy's very cross about that."

Father wasn't there at all, but I didn't miss him and couldn't remember what he looked like, even when I squeezed my eyes tight.

★ ★ ★

Patsy and I shared a bed against one wall, though it wasn't a real bed, just a metal frame with a heavy cloth stretched over it. Mother and Johnny shared a bed opposite. After our train ride and long walk, I felt very tired, but my eyes would not close. I missed my soft pillow, my pink blanket, and Patsy took up too much room. I tried to push her away with my feet, but every time I pushed, Patsy took away the covers and a tug of war started. Mother got cross, told us to behave. "Stop fidgeting," she said. So we learned to share the bed, and on cold nights Patsy made the bed warm and I put my icy toes on her legs.

The next morning, we went shopping, just like at home, except that these shops were not at the top of the street. Mother told Patsy to come with us, she would show her where the shops were. Patsy walked slowly, hands behind back, dragging herself along the street, scuffing her shoes on the pavement, looking for pebbles to kick. "Stop dawdling," Mummy said and gave her a shopping bag to carry. Patsy didn't walk any faster.

We walked past houses with flower gardens, rock gardens, elves and goblins standing guard, a birdbath, a big ginger cat spread out on a window-sill, a small black dog who barked and ran around looking brave. Mummy said to watch out for dogs, they bite, but I like dogs and know they will never bite me.

We went to a vegetable shop, my first one. At home, Fred and his horse Rhubarb came to our street, and sometimes Fred let me give Rhubarb a carrot. Rhubarb didn't snatch it, he sniffed it first, then gently picked it up from my outstretched hand. I loved the feel of his soft nose and the tickles from his whiskers. Our milkman had a horse too, smaller than Rhubarb. I didn't know his name, but every day he let me stroke his soft chest and moved his head up and down in a thank you.

Next stop, a newspaper shop for Mummy's cigarettes, but the old man behind the counter didn't give me a sweet. He had a few stuck to the bottoms of big, smeared glass jars, humbugs and jelly babies. Mr. Dollymore, at the newspaper shop at home, sometimes gave me a sweet wrapped in shiny paper, paper that made a crinkly sound when I twisted it open. He gave me one for my friend Gerald too. Gerald lived next door and we had played almost every morning. There was no one to play with now. I asked Mummy if we could go home. But she told me "There's a war on." Though she never explained "war," so I didn't see why we couldn't go home, unless "war" was something really bad and only happened in London.

★ ★ ★

There was a park nearby, as close as the common at home, and we were off to play there. Mother had taken Johnny and me to the common almost every day after shopping. She would play catch with me, ring around the roses and we would fall down on the grass at the end. Then Mummy would give me a special treat for helping her shop, usually a yummy biscuit.

Tiny white daisies speckled the cool damp grass where we sat for a rest, under the shade of a giant, leafy tree. Johnny tried to catch birds, while I picked daisies and tried to make a necklace. Mummy sat on the grass next to me and helped make holes in the stems with her fingernails, but it was hard to thread them and soon the tiny daisies were sad and soggy in my sweaty fingers.

"Time to go," Mummy said. "Here, Joanie, I'll give you a ride," and showed me how to stand on the bar between the handlebars of Johnny's pram.

The best part of every day in Brighton was when Ted and I played tea party on the two stairs right in the middle of the sun and light, where specks of silver floated down and around us, like fairy dust. "More tea, Ted?" "How is the weather?" Mummy let me use two pretty cups and the milk jug, though it was filled with water, in case I spilled.

I liked to talk with Ted. He always looked at me as if I could understand grown-up things. Ted was older than any grown-up and knew everything.

★ ★ ★

Mother told Patsy to stop moping around, that she could go to the park and take me with her. Patsy tutted and sighed and pushed me towards the door, and down the stairs we went. She was very bossy and told me not to dawdle, that I was a pest, a royal pain and not to expect her to take me every day. I pretended not to hear her, but I did run to keep up.

There were swings in the park and I wanted to swing on the big swings, not the baby boxes. The swings hung from their metal frames, empty and still. Patsy said I'd fall and she'd get in trouble, but I pleaded and held tight to the swing until she lifted me up and plunked me on the wooden seat. "Hold tight," she said, got hold of the chains, pulled me back and let it go – and I swung. "Higher, higher," I yelled. "Right!" she said and pushed hard in the middle of my back. I flew off the swing, onto the gravel. Sharp, tiny rocks dug into my knees and hands. I rubbed them off and saw the dents in my skin, but I didn't cry.

"Told you so, silly billy. You're supposed to hold tight," Patsy said, and helped me up onto the swing again and showed me how to work my legs and body back and forth until I flew by myself. I flew like a bird. I looked up at the sky, at the fluffy clouds and laughed at the tingly scare when the swing came down and felt big, like Patsy. Though Patsy went up 'til her feet touched the sky and she made the chains go bump.

Mummy fussed over me when we got back, poured warm water in a bowl and gently washed my scratched knees and hands, then smoothed on some cream. She gave me a kiss and said, "There, good as new." She didn't scold Patsy, and I was glad.

★ ★ ★

Patsy made friends with Kathleen, our landlady's daughter. Kathleen was big too, with curly hair tied in bunches on either side of her ears, and she was pretty, almost as pretty as Patsy. Patsy's hair was dark and thick and straight, except when Mother wrapped it in strips of cloth, then it was curly, though she only wrapped it for special days. She said it was a "rat's nest," hard enough to comb when straight. Patsy still moped around when Kathleen went to school, but they went to Mass together on Sundays and played after every school day in Kathleen's room.

They wouldn't let me in. I stood outside the brown wooden door and waited – tried to hear what they said, but they whispered behind their hands and, once inside, slammed the door shut so I wouldn't hear.

After dinner and Johnny's nap, Mummy played "Canada" with Johnny and me. We sat on the floor and she told stories about the farm where Patsy, Ted and I would soon be living with our uncles and their chickens and cows. Every day we played Canada. It became my favourite game.

"Are you comfy?" Mummy asked. Sometimes she talked about the ship that would take us for days and days across an ocean, but I liked the part about the animals. "What kind of animals, Mummy?" "Lots of cows, chickens too," she said. "Do you think they have a puppy?" "Oh, yes. I'm sure they do."

And as Mother spoke, I saw it as if I were really there: miles of green fields, big green trees and fat brown cows under cloudless blue skies, and me, running through the grass with a fluffy dog jumping at my side and Ted under my arm.

Johnny only listened for a little while, then staggered around the room, putting things in his mouth, beat Mummy's pots with a spoon and tried to get Ted – that's when he pulled my hair and screamed his favourite words, "No, no, mine, mine." He grabbed my hair and wouldn't let go. Mummy had to cut me free with her scissors. She was very cross and carried Johnny outside and buckled him in his pram. I heard our neighbors stop and give him attention with silly baby talk, which made him stop yelling. Mrs. Jupp gave him biscuits too, which he dribbled all down his clothes and rubbed all over his face.

★   ★   ★

Mother sent Patsy to the bakers and the grocers every day to get her out of her hair. But it was raining, and Patsy had rushed back in a sulk. She was sitting by the window staring at the fat, flat raindrops slipping down the glass. Kathleen had gone to the pictures with her mother that day and Patsy was really grumpy. Her beautiful doll would cheer her up, I thought. Patsy called her doll Mama Jane; she had big gold earrings and a long, frilly dress of red and yellow, and a turban around her head. Mama Jane was very heavy and as I walked towards Patsy, I tripped down the stairs.

"You clumsy brat!" Mama Jane's head was in pieces. My hands shook as I tried to fix her, but Patsy jerked my arms away. "I could just *kill* you," she said, and I believed her. Her eyes were as green as a cat's and she had a temper like a grown-up. I was more terrified of Patsy than sorry I broke her beautiful china doll.

Mother swept the pieces up and Patsy threw all of Mama Jane in the rubbish, her earrings too, and kicked the bin. Mother said, "Now Patsy, it's no use crying over spilt milk." I wondered what milk had to do with a broken doll.

★ ★ ★

Mother and Patsy sat at the table. Mother was reading a letter, her voice soft, almost a whisper. I listened hard and heard bits of words and "Red Cross" over and over.

"I don't care about my classmates, or the stupid nuns, or the stupid boats, stupid government, stupid war!" Patsy yelled. She pushed her chair away from the table and stamped out of the room; she was going to play with Kathleen, she said. "*She* doesn't get shoved around!"

Mother sighed and went to the dresser. She took out Patsy's clothes and placed them on our bed. I sat on the floor, out of the way, and watched as she started packing a suitcase. Mother's face looked tight and I knew not to ask questions. Then she emptied her purse on the table and started counting coins: copper pennies, silver sixpences and shillings, two shillings, half a crowns. Mummy sighed as she tied some silver coins in a hankie and placed it in Patsy's suitcase. I wondered what Patsy would do with so much money. "Here, Joanie, this one's for you," Mummy said, and gave me a pretty farthing with a fat robin on one side. I put it in my matchbox, which held two more. I shook the box and heard the chink, chink, and felt rich.

Then Mother took out her paper money, each note folded into a tiny square, put one on the table and started to write a letter. The letter was folded with the square of money inside and sealed in an envelope, which joined the coins in the suitcase.

"Hello, Patsy," I said when she came back at teatime. She walked past me and sat by the window. Patsy wouldn't talk to anybody; she didn't eat her tea either even though it was our special Sunday tea – soft-boiled egg and buttered bread fingers for dipping, soldiers – and when she got up in the morning, not her breakfast.

"You must eat something," Mummy said. But Patsy turned away and said nothing.

I held Ted out for her to cuddle. He always made me feel better, but she didn't take him. I stayed close in case she changed her mind.

Mummy sighed. "I'll make you a sandwich to eat on the way," she said. Patsy hid the sandwich on the windowsill behind the curtain. She gave me a narrow-eyed look that said, "don't tell!"

"They're here," said Mother as she pinned a luggage label to Patsy's dress. "Hurry up now, Patsy." Mother grabbed the suitcase and pushed Patsy gently towards the door. "Stay here, Joanie, and look after Johnny. Back in a minute. Patsy, your gas mask." Patsy picked up the cardboard box and banged it hard against the door on her way out. We all had gas masks; you weren't allowed to go anywhere without it.

I ran to the window. A black car waited outside, and two ladies were talking to Mother. Patsy climbed in the car. She didn't wave goodbye.

"Don't worry Ted, she's just going for a ride." I kissed his furry face to make him feel better.

Though I missed hearing Patsy breathe, I now had the bed all to myself. Soon I didn't miss her at all in our room at the top of the stairs.

CHAPTER 3

THE LOST CHILDREN

Sometimes, if you stand on the bottom rail of a bridge and lean over to watch the river slipping slowly away beneath you, you will suddenly know everything there is to be known. A.A. Milne

Mummy was washing clothes. She used to sing when she washed clothes, now she smoked cigarettes. Puffs of smoke rose above her head; she leaned back away from it, eyes slanted closed, cigarette dangling at the corner of her mouth. I sat on the step and watched her dry her hands on her apron, take a new cigarette from her pocket, light it from the old and then rub more soap into my vest. Bubbles escaped and melted in the air. Mummy washed clothes in the white enamel basin every day and dried them in the garden downstairs or on the wooden horse placed by the fire. She ironed them too. "Must get the damp out," she told me. I liked to watch the hot iron touch them, hear the hiss, see the damp rising up in the air like a cloud smelling of soap.

Mummy gave me a little white pipe she had bought at the newspaper shop and showed me how to scoop up soapy water and make bubbles. It took a bit to get the hang of it, and I swallowed a lot of soapy water, but I soon had the room full of rainbows. Johnny, sitting on the floor, tried his best to catch them, which made Mummy laugh.

It was very quiet without Patsy, lonely somehow. So I asked Mummy if we could play Canada.

"Um?" she said.

"Can we play Canada?"

"Maybe tomorrow, Joanie, there's lots to do today."

I knew "maybes" never happened. I went to my private place on the big staircase, sat in the rainbow where the fairy dust floated, and whispered Mummy's Canada stories to Ted.

★   ★   ★

Rain poured down, outside was as dark as night, but we had to go shopping. Mummy tied her blue scarf over her head and pulled my hat down low over my ears. She said that it never rained this much in London, that Brighton was a miserable place. I liked the rain – at least I did while my Wellington boots still fit me, then I'd jump in the gutter and watch the water splash, but now they were too small and Mummy couldn't find any more, and the rain ran down my neck and into my shoes.

The butcher was closed, the white marble counter bare, his windows empty. Mummy banged on the glass door, but nobody came. "Blast!" she said. I wasn't allowed to say that word. We walked back home in rain so heavy it looked thick, like milk, as it hit the pavement and bounced up again, wetting whatever it missed coming down. By the time we got back to our room I was shivery cold. Only Johnny was dry, wrapped in his pram with the hood up and cover clipped to the sides and front.

"Let's have toast for tea," Mummy said as she hung up our wet clothes. She dried me with a soft towel until my skin tingled, squeezed the rain out of my hair, dusted me with her special powder and slipped my nightie over my head. Then she put a kettle on the hotplate, lit the gas fire and wove thick slices of bread onto a brass toasting fork. The fire's white face soon turned orange, then red – that's when it was ready to make toast. I sat on a cushion in front of the gas fire, my fluffy slippers warming my toes, and breathed in the smell of toasty bread as the warmth from the fire took away the cold from my bones. Mummy pulled me towards her, her arm around my shoulders, while I sipped a cup of steaming, milky-sweet tea and slowly chewed the soft, buttery toast and pretended it was a real fire, with orange and blue and white flames.

As soon as we had finished, Mummy was busy again, washing, ironing, cleaning, polishing, smoking her cigarettes, reading the paper…and quiet. "I can help you, Mummy," I said. Mummy smiled and reminded me of the last time I'd helped. We had been cleaning windows when the milkman rang the doorbell. While Mummy went to talk with him, I picked up her cloth, put her cigarette in my mouth and proceeded to lean out the window. "You gave me such a fright," she laughed. "I thought you were going to fall." She rumpled my hair and gave me the tea towels to fold. I matched up all the corners and folded them in squares. I felt big and important.

★ ★ ★

"Joanie, you must keep away from the windows and never touch the curtains," Mummy said every evening as she drew the thick curtains together. "It's 'blackout' time." That night I forgot. The rain had stopped and I wanted to show Ted the black sky with white holes made by bright stars and I parted the curtains just enough for his head to poke out.

"Get away from that window, it's blackout time!" I jumped back, my skin crawled, my eyes prickled with tears. Mummy had never yelled at me before. "Blackout" must be terrible.

"Didn't mean to make you jump, Joanie," Mummy said, and gave me a hug, then tucked me in bed. I was almost asleep when a screaming sound filled the room, my body, and stabbed my ears. I scrambled out of bed, heart thumping, legs shaking. It was so dark.

"Mummy," I stumbled towards her bed.

"Shush," she said, "you'll wake up Johnny. It's only the sirens." She said that the sirens were just practicing. But when I asked her why, she didn't answer, she just said "Shush." She cuddled me until I stopped shaking, tucked me back in my bed and smoothed my face.

★ ★ ★

"Happy birthday, Joanie," said Mummy, and she tied a big pink ribbon in my hair. I was four, just like that, in one day. We had tinned peaches and biscuits with jam inside and icing on top for tea and sang the Birthday Song.

Mrs. Jupp gave Mother the biscuits. After I'd finished my birthday tea and licked all the peach juice off my plate, Mummy said, "You're a big girl now. You can go to Patsy's school soon. Won't that be nice?"

Canada had become like a fairy story – not quite real, more a dream. My stomach turned to jelly, like when the sirens screamed. I tried to tell her I didn't want to go, but she interrupted. "It won't be forever," she said, "only until all the lights go on again."

I sat on the steps in the rainbow and whispered to Ted. "Don't worry Ted, we'll sail over the ocean and live on a farm with Patsy. It won't be forever."

★ ★ ★

Spring tried to push winter away and tiny green buds covered the black branches of the trees outside our window. We hadn't walked to the piers in a long time, and Mummy said we would go for a special treat. "It's a lovely day for the seaside," she said.

Rolls of twisted, spiky wire stood on guard in front of the water as far as I could see. We didn't walk out on the pier. Mummy said they were broken, both of them. They were, too – the parts that went out over the sea were gone, like a giant wave had gobbled them up. Holding Ted tight, I grabbed the side of Johnny's pram and stared at the jagged ends of the pier. The black, hungry water banged and pushed against the posts, making me shiver.

"What are those, Mummy?" I pointed to some large brown boxes standing on the shiny pebbles. Patsy had told me about guns, and somehow, I knew the answer, so when Mummy said they were guns, I wasn't surprised and didn't want to know more.

The wind blew hard off the sea and by the time we got home, I was shivery cold, so Mummy stood me in the huge bathtub while she ran the warm water and poured it over me. "There," she said, "that should take the chill off," and wrapped me in her big towel and rubbed me warm.

"Yoo-hoo." It was Mrs. Jupp "Join me in a cuppa?" she said, knocking on the door. She had a tea tray with biscuits on a pretty plate. Mummy took it from her and put it on the table and told her we were just back from the broken piers.

"No, haven't been there since they blew them up, haven't the heart. Such a shame, they were lovely piers," Mrs. Jupp said to Mummy. "Beaches are mined now too. Never mind."

They talked quietly and looked at me a lot. Mrs. Jupp gave me a biscuit with jam inside and I opened it up and scraped the lovely red stickiness from the center before I nibbled at the sweet covers.

The next day, Mother started packing, this time for me. I watched her put my clothes in a small leather case, all except my blue woolen leggings that matched my coat and the little blue hat that went with it. Mummy said they were too small now, wouldn't last another winter. Except for talking about my leggings, she didn't speak, didn't say where I was going, but I knew she had finally remembered. I was to live with Patsy in Canada.

I thought she had forgotten. I had hoped she had. I certainly had. It was fun here with Mummy, especially without Patsy to boss me around. "I don't want to go away. I want to stay with you. I'll be good. I promise. Please, Mummy!" That's what I wanted to say, but I just stood and watched. My throat hurt. My hands were shaky. I felt cold all over.

"Yoo-hoo," our landlady called from the hall. Mrs. Jupp was going to take care of Johnny, Mummy told me as she tied my shoes. Then Mummy tied a brown luggage label to my best blue coat, the one with the soft velvet collar. Mummy was very quiet tying the string. I began to worry if I was going to get lost. I clutched Ted tighter.

We walked to the train station where the four of us had arrived such a long time ago and waited for our train. I heard the whistle first, then saw the round black face of the train, which screeched to a stop and sighed with a puff of steam rising from the tracks. We climbed into a stuffy carriage smelling of smoke and filled with soldiers (do they ride trains all day?). Mummy had to lift me up the last step – it was very high – and one of the soldiers grabbed my arm. "'Ere yer go, luv," he said. He had a moustache. Straps hung from his shoulders and bags stood between his boots. His teeth were brown, he smelt like the chimney-sweep man – sour and smoky. I turned away, leaned into my mother and clutched Ted tighter.

He leaned closer to me, "Shy, are yer, pet?" I held my breath and clenched my eyes shut. Mummy sat me on her lap and told the soldier that I was just a bit quiet that day, that's all.

More soldiers climbed onto the train at the next stop, and with their guns and bags and big boots, soon crowded the corridor and filled up our carriage, covering up the windows, stepping on each other's toes, so all I could see was brown, all I could breathe was yucky cigarette smoke.

Mummy said it was time to get off, that we would catch a bus now. While it felt good to breathe fresh air again, I wondered why we were to get on a bus. I thought we were going on a boat. But the bus was there, as if waiting for us. It was filled with children. We rode in silence, past dark green treetops and tangled telephone wires. Some of the big boys jumped around and made noise, but most of us were very quiet. I held Ted tight and pushed myself against my mother and wondered if these children were going on the boat too.

When the bus finally stopped, there was not a boat to be seen. Instead of an ocean, buildings stretched out along the road. I turned in a circle. "Mummy, where's the ocean?" Without saying a word, without looking at me, she grabbed my hand and started walking towards a large building. "Mummy, where is the boat?"

Children filled the dark, bare building carrying suitcases, paper bags, gas masks...crying, fighting, screaming...silent. Grown-ups called off names from lists and stood children against the walls. Children with wet, white faces.

Why am I here with all these lost children?

CHAPTER 4

THE CUPBOARD
UNDER THE STAIRS

If ever there is tomorrow when we're not together, there is some-thing you must always remember: you are braver than you believe, stronger than you seem, and smarter than you think. But the most important thing is, even if we're apart, I'll always be with you.
A.A. Milne

Mummy had played Canada every day in our room at the top of the stairs, so why were we in this ugly, crowded, noisy place? She had never said, "We'll see," like she did when I really wouldn't get the biscuit or go to the swings. She had said, "*When* you are with your uncles in Canada, you can feed the chickens and cows." She always said "when" if it was true.

"Where's the farm?" Tugging at her coat, I yelled, "Mummy, where are the animals?"

She held tight to my sweaty hand and pushed through the crowd. "Look, Joanie, Patsy's over there," she said. I didn't care. I clung to my mother's coat, tried to hide. She kept walking, dragging me with her.

Noises echoed in my ears. I couldn't speak. I hardly noticed Patsy. Mummy pulled her hand away from mine and said, "Here's Patsy. Hush now, don't cry, be brave." I grabbed her coat with both hands and buried my face in its rose-scented folds. She bent down, held my shoulders and pulled me loose. She kissed me goodbye on my wet cheek. A kiss that didn't feel warm.

"Here's a pretty hankie," she said, pinning her hankie to my coat. She draped my cardboard gas mask case around my neck and put my suitcase on the floor.

"I'll take over," said a lady. I saw her shoes first, brown with laces – she was very tall. "It's better if you just leave."

"Joanie, you mustn't cry, you must be good and brave," she told me, turned around and disappeared.

She left. Mummy left. I couldn't see her. The lady held me tight, I wanted to bite her, kick her, and I wriggled until I was free. Big boys, more ladies with brown stockings and big shoes, blocked my way. My gas mask was heavy around my neck. Somebody bumped me. Ted fell. I pushed, I clawed, I crawled between shoes, boots…my fingers, I can't lift my hand. I bit the boy's leg, he moved. Ted. I clutched him… *run fast, run away. Mummy's gone. Poor Ted.*

Be quiet – hide, hide under that chair – stop crying. I crawled under a wooden chair; nobody would find me there.

"Come along now." The big-shoed lady stood me up. "Be brave."

I hugged Ted with all my might. I couldn't be brave. I didn't want to be brave! *"Why?"* There must be a mistake – something's gone wrong. Mummy never broke promises.

Grown-ups with their lists gave me answers: "There are no boats." "Perhaps the boat will come another day." I knew they weren't telling the truth – you can tell from people's eyes when they are not telling the truth, the way they look back and forth at each other to see if they should say more.

Patsy came up beside me – she grabbed my arm. I pulled hard to get away. I had to find my mother. She must be here, somewhere.

"Let me go," I screamed. I tried to kick her legs. I wanted to scratch her hands.

"You're being a horror!" she said, shaking me like she shook the tablecloth.

Then, "I'm sorry, don't cry," when I screamed louder. She pushed the hair away from my wet face and told me we would live together with a nice lady, "Standing right over there, Mrs. Croft." I didn't want to live with a nice lady. I didn't want to live with Patsy either. I wanted my mother.

"Move along now," the big-shoed lady said. Patsy dragged me through the crowd. "All the ships are broken," Patsy said. "Everyone's moving away from the bombs." I kept on crying.

"We'll have a foster mother." I cried louder.

Patsy had been placed with an elderly couple that lived in a small cottage on the edge of town and near her school. They were willing to take me in, too, Patsy said. Mr. and Mrs. Croft were their names, and I was about to meet Mrs. Croft.

"She's a nice lady, you'll like her," Patsy said.

"I don't care. I want to live on the farm in Canada," I yelled and dug my heels into the floor.

Patsy bent down and pulled me in front of her. "Well you can't! Now stop carrying on, you're embarrassing me. You're lucky Mrs. Croft wants you. There are plenty of children she could take if she wanted. And if you don't shut up, nobody will want you and you'll be left here alone all night long in the dark."

I looked around the room. Children were leaving with grown-ups, but they were all big like Patsy. Children my size were sitting on chairs, waiting. Patsy gave me a shove towards Mrs. Croft.

I saw her black, laced up shoes first; her black coat almost touched them. She looked very old, round and short, her white hair pulled back from her wrinkled face, and no lipstick. Not at all pretty like my mother. She didn't smell like roses either. She bent down, took hold of my hand. Smiling, she said, "Hello, dear," and then, "There, there, dearie, don't cry, it's all right. I'm your foster mother. Let's go home." She looked at Ted and asked, "Now who's this then?" I looked down at Ted. His head was wet from my tears, his fur stood up in spikes, but I felt better seeing his face.

"Come on, dear. That's a good girl. I have some nice strawberry jam at home." Her voice was quiet, soothing. I heard only her, all the crying and yelling around me silenced by her gentleness. I held her hand; her touch was soft, her skin was rough. She gave my hand a squeeze. Light shone on her sticky-out hair – it looked silver, like the fairy godmother in my picture book at home. Clutching Ted really hard, I stopped crying.

★　★　★

Her cottage looked old, like Mrs. Croft; it smelled like her, too, and like the cellar at home where the coal was stored – damp darkness. The kitchen window was very small and criss-crossed with tape, but a fire in the black iron fireplace made the room bright and cheery. Mr. Croft stood up from his fat chair and smiled. He looked just like Mrs. Croft – old and bent and kind.

Mrs. Croft asked if I was thirsty. I wanted to please her and said, "Yes." And would I like water? "Yes." She sat me on the wooden draining board alongside the kitchen sink and gave me first one, then two, then three glasses of water, and said, "There's a good girl," after each one. I wanted to please her even more. I had never sat on a draining board, or remembered drinking cold water before, and though my stomach was ready to pop, she seemed so impressed with my capacity for water that I didn't want to disappoint her and gave up only when, to my relief, she said I could have more after tea.

"Patsy," I said, tugging her skirt, "I need to go to the toilet."

She sighed, grabbed my hand and into the garden we went to a wooden shed right at the back. "It's in there, hurry up, I'm cold."

But it was dark inside and smelly, too. The floor was earth and a board with a hole in the center waited for my bottom. "Patsy…."

"What!"

"I don't like it in here."

"Too bad. I don't like it either. Just hurry up!"

Patsy was getting cross, so I had no choice but to climb up onto the damp board. Pieces of newspaper lay beside me. They were scratchy.

★　★　★

We all sat at a round table covered in a flowery cloth. A teapot sat in the center and wore a cozy in the shape of a marmalade-coloured cat, and we chewed soft white bread smothered with strawberry jam and drank sweet, steaming tea. My tear-stained face and sticky hands were washed in a bowl of warm water as I sat on a kitchen chair by the crackling fire. My nightie was waiting on a wooden rack, getting warmed, and my foster mother stood in front of me, took off my dress and pulled my nightie over my head. She dusted me first with sweet-smelling powder. Just like Mummy.

With Patsy leading the way, we went to our small bed, which was placed in the cupboard under the stairs.

"Safest part of the house in case of bombs," Mr. Croft said.

I didn't know what bombs were and was too tired to ask. But it certainly looked cozy. The door was gone, and the bed fit tight in the sloping cupboard, like a bird's nest in a tree branch. A bright, patchwork quilt covered it, and the pillowcase was covered in blue flowers.

But it was dark against the wall. Dark places hid things too horrible for the light. Mummy always gave me a nightlight, floating in a saucer of water, and I made a fuss. I wanted to sleep on the outside of the bed where the firelight shone and flickered around the walls. Patsy said, "Oh all right. Just for tonight," moved over and patted the bed.

Cuddling Ted tight, I whispered in his ear, "Don't worry Ted, Mrs. Croft likes you. And maybe we will go to Canada." I kissed his soft face goodnight and started my prayers.

CHAPTER 5

FAREWELL TED

I used to believe in forever…but forever was too good to be true.
A.A. Milne

Mummy's sweeping. I sat up in bed, but it wasn't Mummy cleaning the grate. Mrs. Croft walked towards me, wiping her hands on her apron.

"'Morning dearie, have a good night's sleep then?" I nodded and clutched Ted.

"Come and have some breakfast."

I was very hungry. Hands behind back, holding my Ted, I walked to the table and waited for the invitation to sit.

"Don't be shy," she said, "you sit here next to me. Patsy still sleeping?"

"Yes," I said mouth full of sticky strawberry jam. "Mummy said Patsy would sleep all day if she let her."

"I heard that, tattletale," said Patsy. I pulled my arms in tight, ready for the pinch.

Patsy ate her breakfast quickly and dressed for school. "Glad you found some of your old friends, dear," said Mrs. Croft as Patsy left, slamming the door behind her. Mrs. Croft didn't scold Patsy for slamming the door, she just sighed.

★   ★   ★

All the cottage windows were small and taped crisscross. Sunshine didn't come inside. It was so dark, I could barely see the pattern on the wallpaper, but Mrs. Croft had one large picture on her kitchen wall where the light shone in from the tiny window.

"Look, Ted," I showed him the picture. There was a boy, a girl and two soldiers dressed in armor, one sat at a table, an orange in his hand, the other had a long, pointed stick and stood behind him. The girl's hair was fair, like mine, and her dress was green. Apart from two black-and-white china dogs on the mantelpiece, this picture was the only thing of interest around and I wanted to know what it meant.

Mrs. Croft said the soldiers were searching for the children's father, and asking, "Where is your father?" The girl was standing in front of her little brother, protecting him. She wanted that orange, but I knew she wouldn't tell. The men had angry faces and I knew they were bad.

"She's very brave, Ted."

★   ★   ★

Mr. Croft was digging in the backyard. "Digging a Victory garden, putting in some nice veggies," he told me. "See that worm there? Mind him now." The worm was pink and clean. "Nothing grows without worms and bees."

"You'll get right messy out there," Mrs. Croft said, "come inside, I have something nice to tell you."

Maybe Mummy is coming to take me home. Maybe I am going to Canada. I ran inside. "You can go to school with Patsy tomorrow. The nuns said so. Aren't you a lucky girl?" I didn't know if I wanted to go to school and wasn't sure why I should feel lucky. If my mother was coming to fetch me, I'd feel lucky.

"It's a lovely school, is St. Anne's."

"Patsy goes to Sacred Hearts."

"Well, I don't know about that, she's in St. Anne's now with all her schoolmates."

I sat Ted on my lap and whispered about school. It might be fun. Mrs. Croft was too old to play. I'd get to be with Patsy, too. We agreed, when Patsy came home, we'd ask her about St. Anne's.

"It's the stupid war," Patsy said. "Sacred Heart's moved here. Everyone came. We're lumped together in St. Anne's Convent. I hate it!"

"But is it fun?"

"School's never fun, it's plain boring."

I woke up early, butterflies in my stomach. Mrs. Croft brushed my hair and helped me put on my best clothes and clean white socks. I had three pair. (We had to have three pair, Mummy said. "One to wear, one for spare, one in the wash." That was the rule.) We had porridge for breakfast, with sugar on top.

"Open up," Mrs. Croft said as she put two bottles on the table. "This'll make you big and strong." She gave me first a spoonful of yucky cod-liver oil, then a yummy dose of thick, golden orange juice. Mummy had done the same every day. She'd said the same thing too.

"Off you go then." I picked up Ted and held him under my arm.

"Oh no, dearie, he can't go."

"But…"

"Sorry, dearie, the nuns won't allow it."

Poor Ted. I lay him back in bed and pulled the covers up to his nose. We had never been apart before, except when it rained too hard and he might get soaked outside. I kissed his fluffy head and promised I would be back soon.

"Here, you can't go without this," Mrs. Croft said, and hung the cardboard box with my gas mask in it around my neck. I held it tight and tried not to worry about Ted.

Patsy took my hand and we walked down the lane and past some fields with long green grass shining wet in the soft sun. I looked at the trees and their moving branches that made a swishing sound, like rain falling. Patsy jerked my arm. "Stop dawdling, we'll be late," she said, "then you'll see how much fun school is."

Other girls hurried past us and into a brick building. A statue of a beautiful lady stood in front of it – she wore a long pink and blue dress and carried flowers in her arms. Her face was kind, and she smiled at me.

"You wait for me after school right here," Patsy said. "No running off."

We walked towards a nun, tall and thin. I knew she was a nun because of her strange black clothes.

"This your sister, Patricia?"

Patsy nodded. "Come with me, child." And with her fingers on top of my head, the nun walked me into a classroom, where Patsy had told me all the "babies" sat. Girls were squashed tight together, sharing desks. "This is Sister Theresa," the tall, thin nun said, nodding her head towards the nun standing by the blackboard, holding a long stick in her hand. Sister Theresa stared at me over her fat cheeks, through her thick glasses, tapped a chair in the front row. "Sit," she said. With my cardboard box on my lap, I sat.

"Repeat after me," Sister Theresa began, and holding her black rosary beads in her hand, started saying prayers. Her voice sounded angry. She walked back and forth along the rows of girls, thumping heads with her knuckles and saying, "Pay attention." I moved my lips and tried to remember the words as I listened to her footsteps and waited for the thump.

A bell rang. "Break time. No running, no screeching and keep off the grass," she said, and with one sound, all the chairs scraped back on the floor and the girls rushed out the door. It was over. *Maybe we will go home after break time and I can cuddle Ted.* With that happy thought, I followed the girls outside. Some of them played together. They wore uniforms and must be friends, I thought. The rest of us stood around and stared at the ground, at the girls playing, anywhere but each other.

Ladies with aprons walked around the black-topped playground and gave us each a small bottle of milk and a sandwich. I didn't feel hungry and left mine for the birds.

The sound of a whistle brought us all back into the classroom again, and while I couldn't tell time, I watched the black hand click, click, click slowly around the short black lines of the round white clock while Sister Theresa made us repeat the alphabet to the beat of her cane on her desk. I noticed the rolls of skin under her chin, the tight band of stiff, starched white cloth that seemed to choke her and wondered if it hurt. Maybe that's why she was so grumpy.

Then she told us a story about Jesus, how His hands and feet had nails banged into them, how thirsty He was as He hung from the cross, how He forgave everyone for hurting Him. She held up the crucifix on the end of her rosary and walked around the room so we could all see, and there He was, His head hanging down, so thin, so sad. How awful. Poor Jesus.

"Kiss His feet," she told me. I didn't want to. One foot was nailed on top of the other and bones showed through His skin. She stood there, holding poor Jesus in front of me. I shivered and bent my head and pretended to touch His broken feet with my lips. I could barely wait to hold Ted and tell him about school and that he wouldn't like it.

Sister Theresa rang the bell on her desk two times. "Class dismissed," she said.

Girls walked past me as I waited by the statue. Where was Patsy? Maybe she forgot me. I'd just have to find my own way back to Ted. I remembered the field. But Patsy said I had to wait here. There were only a few girls now walking slowly out to the street. Where was she? I felt a pinch on my arm.

"Well, how do you like school?" Patsy asked.

"It's not fun."

Patsy laughed and got hold of my hand. "Not to worry, Joanie-pony, we'll have fun later."

Patsy walked very slowly, and I wanted to run to Ted. We came to the crossroad to our lane. "Look right, look left, then look right again," Patsy said. But there were no cars, not even a bicycle. I shifted my weight from foot to foot. "Pay attention," she told me and said the words again. "I need the toilet," I cried, "right now!" But she didn't seem to hear me. At last, we started to cross the road, and I felt a warm trickle down my legs and into my shoes. I started to cry and ran ahead of Patsy. Mrs. Croft would be angry, she wouldn't want me anymore. I had to explain.

Patsy unlatched the garden gate and I ran past her into the house, sobbing, "It was an accident, I didn't mean it, I'm a big girl, I'm sorry," and I waited for the scolding, shaking from fear. Mrs. Croft said "There, there," walked me to the fire, took off my knickers and socks and washed and dried my legs, then dressed me in my clean undies. "That's better," she said, and it was.

I went to the cupboard under the stairs and picked up Ted. I held him close under my chin and shut my eyes. He was so soft and warm I could feel it all over, as if he cuddled me. I heard my mother say, "You mustn't cry, Joanie, you must be good and brave."

"You won't like school, Ted," I whispered and told him about the angry nuns and the slow click, click of the clock.

★ ★ ★

"Did you read stories today?" Mrs. Croft asked.

"Sister Theresa told stories about Jesus. He was very poor and suffered a lot."

"Well, I don't know about that, but after tea, I'll tell you a nice story," she said.

We sat around the table and had thick slices of bread and jam, boiled carrots – from "my Victory Garden," announced Mr. Croft – and hot, milky tea. Patsy helped clear the table and Mr. Croft rolled up his shirt-sleeves to wash the dishes.

"Come sit here, dearie," Mrs. Croft said, patting her lap. I didn't remember sitting on Mummy's lap and felt shy. But I climbed up and she pulled me close and began a fairy story about the Princess and the Pea. Nestled between Ted and Mrs. Croft, I didn't hear the end.

"Tired out," I heard Mrs. Croft say as I was led to bed.

★ ★ ★

Patsy and I walked to and from school every day. Of course, she was in a different classroom, but we were together for Mass every morning. Mass was boring, except when the boy swung the golden ball and sweet smoke rose in the air. I wondered if when I was bigger, I would be allowed to do that, too. Patsy said no because I was a girl. It seemed only boys got to wear the white frock and hold the golden ball.

We dawdled home and Patsy chatted with her friends. They talked grown-up things like how handsome Roy Rogers was, how his eyes sparkled. They all seemed to know him, so he must have been their friend, though I never met him. They talked about songs too, and though I didn't understand half of what they said, being with Patsy was almost like being big.

Every day, I ran into the cottage and picked up Ted, closed my eyes and cuddled him. He felt soft and warm as he melted into me. Then I'd tell him about my day. "Jill got caned today," I told him, still trembling with fear at the sight of Sister Theresa's angry face, the way her chins wiggled and the sound of Jill's cries as the stick sliced into her hands, one, two, three. And I knew Ted wouldn't let anybody cane me.

★   ★   ★

On one of our walks from school, we saw soldiers jump out of an airplane and parachute down from the sky into a field, floating like dandelion seeds when blown from their stems for wishes.

"Why not let Ted have a ride like that?" Patsy said. I had to admit, it did look like fun. But I was fearful he would get hurt, or worse yet, lost.

"It's not the least bit dangerous," she said, "the soldiers wouldn't do it if it was. Besides, Ted deserves some fun."

Ted had been a very good friend to me for as long as I could remember, longer than Patsy, or even my mother. He made me feel brave too. I just whispered my fears in his fluffy ear, and he would take them away.

"Come on, Joanie-pony."

Mr. and Mrs. Croft were out, and before I could stop her, Patsy picked up Ted, and up the stairs she went. I rushed after her, not sure what to do. The bedroom was tiny and dark, with one little window pushed open. Patsy tied her hankie to Ted's arms. She pulled a chair up to the window.

"Come on," she said, handing me Ted. I looked into his dark-brown, glass eyes and thought I saw a tear. He didn't want to go on a ride. I held him tight.

"Patsy, he might get dirty."

Patsy tutted, "Don't be silly. He won't get dirty and he can't break. Hurry up, before Mrs. Croft comes home."

I climbed onto the wiggly seat, grabbing the windowsill with my hand. The sun was shining, the sky so blue.

"Here, I'll help you." Her hand fit all round his body.

But I couldn't let Ted go. I was afraid of losing him – he did, after all, have only one leg, which might get him in trouble on landing. I didn't want to do it. But I knew Patsy would get angry soon and call me a crybaby. And he did deserve to have some fun.

I turned Ted's face to mine, held him tight and covered his face in quick kisses.

"Have a nice ride," I told him, and on Patsy's count of one, two, three, she let him go and off he went – not down into the garden below where Patsy said he would, but out and away, floating on that breeze over the high, wooden, garden fences. I stood on my tiptoes, leaned out the window, called his name, tried to see where he would land. I could count. It looked like four fences away.

Scrambling down from the chair, I sat on my bottom and slid down the stairs. "Ted, Ted here I am." I had to find him. I'd knock on doors and ask if I could look in the gardens. I could prove he was mine. Patsy grabbed my hand. I pulled away, screaming, "Ted, Ted." She wrapped her arms around me. I kicked and struggled to break free.

"Shush," she said. "Be quiet, stop fussing, it's only a scruffy toy."

"I want my Ted," I screamed as loud as I could. "Let me go!"

But she held me tight. Patsy was scared of getting into trouble for being where we were not allowed and losing a perfectly good hankie. She didn't care about Ted, not one bit.

"What's all this then?" asked Mrs. Croft as she walked into the house. Patsy had to tell her what had happened. But there were only words of comfort: "Oh, don't worry, dearie, I'm sure he's all right," and "Perhaps we can find another toy," which really proved nobody understood the magic that was Ted.

"Please, let me find him." I grabbed Mrs. Croft's apron and held it tight. She patted my head, "Sorry, dearie, it's just not safe."

"I'll look both ways when I cross the street. I know where he is, just four gardens away. I'll be nice to the grown-ups. I won't cry or make a fuss."

Mrs. Croft sighed a long sigh before saying "Sorry, dearie."

Why? I wanted to scream the word so everyone would hear me. *Why?*

My hands shook, my face burned. I heard my mother's voice, "You must be good and brave, Joanie. We don't want to make trouble. We're evacuees."

I tried being brave – Ted would have expected it. But I missed my mother, and I wanted to be in Canada. Ted wouldn't get lost in Canada.

I walked to the cupboard under the stairs and sat on the bed. I held my breath to get rid of my hiccups and looked at Ted's place – the covers were rumpled from Patsy picking him up in such a hurry for his ride.

Poor Ted. He was out there all alone, and I couldn't help him. It was teatime but I wasn't hungry. Then it was bedtime. Who would protect me all night, and who would make bad things better? How could I sleep now that Ted was gone? The tears wouldn't stop. My hair stuck to my face and my ears tickled from their overflow.

Patsy sat on our bed, "Go to sleep, Pet," she said, using her special name for me. But I imagined all kinds of terrible things about Ted: he had landed in a pile of leaves and would be buried and burned with them, he had fallen into a tree and would get ruined from the rain.

Would he miss me? Who would hug him now? My arms were empty. My insides hurt.

★   ★   ★

Our foster parents had no children of their own. I thought perhaps that was why they were so kind. We were their first children. But somehow, somewhere, Mrs. Croft had managed to find a dark-brown Mickey Mouse. She gave him to me saying, "Here, dearie, Mickey will help you sleep."

He was small, almost too small to cuddle, but he would just have to do, and holding my new friend close to my chest, I sobbed myself to sleep.

When I woke up, he was nowhere to be seen. I looked under the covers, on the floor – nothing – he had just disappeared. Patsy pointed to a brown sludge on my nightie and told me that was him. How could that be? Patsy was always teasing. I asked Mrs. Croft if she would help me find him. She told me the same thing. It seemed he was a chocolate Mickey Mouse.

"I tried to take him when you was asleep dearie, but you held him so tight," Mrs. Croft said.

CHAPTER 6

BREAD AND CHEESE

They went to a Fair, and they all won prizes—
Three plum puddidngses and three mince-pieses.
They rode on elephants and swang on swingses,
And hit three coco-nuts at coco-nut shieses. A.A. Milne

"**T**ed," I whispered. But he wasn't there. I did not want to go to school with those angry nuns.

Patsy pinched my arm, "Hurry up, you'll make me late." I sat on the bed in my nightie and refused to budge.

"What's this then?" asked Mrs. Croft. She told me not to cry, that she would have a surprise for me when I came home and helped me get dressed.

"Come on, Joanie, I've got something special to show you today," said Patsy and, grabbing my hand, she pulled me out the door. I dragged my gas mask case behind me and walked as slow as I could. I didn't want to make Patsy happy. Not one bit.

We walked along the lane and, as Patsy didn't nag me to hurry up, I found myself walking faster. And there, in one of the open fields, which had been just a field the day before, shiny horses grazed. Caravans painted green, with huge bright flowers decorating the sides, their doors wide open, stood as if they had been there forever, and children laughed and played on the green grass. Their clothes, blue, red, yellow dazzled in the sunlight and moved as freely as the children dancing in their bare feet. My clothes didn't move at all, except to brush my knees when I walked. They were stiff and dull, like Patsy's.

The grown-ups too, were noisy, talking and laughing while setting up striped tents. All the other grown-ups I saw were serious, grumpy – especially the nuns – and nobody wore colourful clothes; they wore black or brown or grey

"They're gypsies," said Patsy.

I stood and stared. How I wanted to live in a bright caravan, wear bright clothes, run in the grass, laugh. I didn't want to leave. Patsy said we would stop by again on the way home.

"Look, they have puppies," I said, pointing to five or six round, spotted balls of fluff jumping around the children. But Patsy just kept walking. I kept my eyes on the cuddly puppies as long as I could.

The day dragged by, the clock went click, click and I thought of the gypsy children who didn't have to go to school, who played in the fields with puppies and horses. That day, I managed to get two thumps on my head for not paying attention. My head sank into my shoulders with each thump.

Patsy met me at the beautiful statue and we hurried back to the field. Patsy said she would play a game and win a present for me. Maybe something to cuddle, I thought, as I trotted along on tiptoes, straining to see over the hedge. I looked around but couldn't see the children or the puppies. It was very quiet there now. Everyone was having tea, I thought.

"Maybe they have a doll," Patsy said. "We have to pay to play. And get our money's worth." Patsy pulled out her hankie where she tied her pennies. She looked at all the tents. There were no toys, but Patsy said she had found *the* prize – a huge chocolate Easter egg wrapped in coloured sparkling paper. My stomach growled as it waited to be fed. Seems it was always empty.

The game was "Bowl Over the Coconuts." Patsy went to the back of the tent, picked up a flap and looked in.

"What yer think yer doing?" a huge man yelled. He just appeared from nowhere. He wore a waistcoat over his collarless shirt, its sleeves rolled up to show his huge, hairy arms. His eyes were narrow and mean.

"We want to play," Patsy said. She wasn't scared of him at all. Patsy just gave her pennies and took aim. All the coconuts fell. I jumped up and down. My sister could do anything. The man restacked the coconuts, ignoring us.

"I want my prize," said Patsy.

"Clear off," the man who took her pennies growled and pushed Patsy's shoulder hard. His face was dark, angry. Patsy tossed her hair, grabbed my wrist and started to walk away. She glanced over her shoulder and made a quick turn behind his tent, finger to lips, opened the flap and reached in for the egg.

"Run!" she yelled. We ran until we came to the lane leading home. Patsy stood holding her side, panting, laughing. My legs were shaking.

"Here, Joanie, this will cheer you up." Patsy tore off the shiny paper, revealing a green Easter egg, chocolate lines showing in the little indented markings. "It's moldy," she said. "That cheating old bugger!" And threw the egg into the bushes.

Little birds screeched as they flew into the air, away from the green-brown missile. I wondered why we couldn't eat it, and said so, more than once, louder and louder.

"I'm sorry," Patsy said, and put her arm around my shoulder. She hadn't done that before, ever. It felt nice. "Are you hungry?" I nodded. I was always hungry. "Pick the leaves off that hedge, the hawthorn bush, that one over there with the dark leaves. They taste just like bread and cheese, and we'll have a picnic."

They were small, shiny green leaves. I picked some and chewed and chewed; they were tough and bitter. I knew I must have eaten cheese but couldn't remember the taste. They certainly did not taste like bread.

"Don't swallow them," she said. So I kept chewing all the way back to the cottage before spitting them out, and with the chewing, forgot my hunger, forgot the egg.

I ran to our bed, hoping Ted had found his way home; instead a tiny doll about the size of my hand lay on the pillow. I picked her up. She was made from different coloured wool, her pink face stitched in a smile. Though she was too tiny to cuddle, it would be nice to carry her around for company, hidden in a pocket or up my sleeve.

"Like your new friend, then?" Mrs. Croft said.

I did. I'd wait to give her a name. Names took a while to think up. I hoped Ted wouldn't mind, and I closed my eyes tight and whispered to him that this was just a doll, he would always be my friend.

I sat on the bed, staring at the tiny doll, and cried inside for Ted. I could see him when I closed my eyes. I saw that his nose was wearing off, some of the black stitches were gone, and his tummy wasn't as fluffy as his arms. I'd never noticed when I'd held him. I felt tears squeeze out of my eyes, run down my face. Did he always have one leg?

"Want me to tell you a story?" Patsy asked. She had never told me a story. I wiped my face on my sleeve, squirmed back on the bed and nestled against the wall.

"That's not the way it goes," I said when Patsy told me Rapunzel's hair fell out when the prince started climbing. "You should see your face." Patsy laughed. She laughed and told me I was a silly billy when I said the same thing about the giant caterpillar eating Jack's beanstalk and causing him to fall down. The only really good story Patsy told was Cinderella. She always said the same words and it always had a happy ending.

★ ★ ★

The next morning, I was up extra early, ready to see the gypsies.

"All right, all right. Pest!" Patsy said as I tugged at her and begged to leave.

Out the door we went, to the field of colours and happy sounds. Bits and pieces of rubbish blew around in the wind, but other than that the field was empty, silent. "Where are they, Patsy?"

"Chased off, I expect."

"Why?"

"People just don't like gypsies hanging around. Trouble follows them, that's what people say, and they steal things."

It was true about Patsy's pennies, but why would they be sent away? Where did they go? The sun was shining, but it had nothing to sparkle under its bright light, no colours except green. The wind blew, but only the trees and rubbish moved. I held onto the fence. Maybe if I stood there long enough, I'd see them all again.

"Come on you, they won't be back, they're gone!"

"But *why?*" Patsy sighed and pulled my hand off the fence, and away I shuffled from the magical field to the school with the grumpy nuns.

Patsy took me on different walks home from school after that, looking for the best shortcut, she said. Some were just alleys running between people's back gardens. On one such walk, Patsy noticed a beautiful apple tree, dripping in fruit, standing alone in the middle of a garden in front of a large, dark house. A high, wooden fence surrounded the garden – at least to me it was high. We went that way all week.

On the last day when we reached the apple tree house, Patsy told me to wait. She scrambled over the fence and jumped up at the branches of the tree. She pulled them towards her and tore off round, rosy apples. I watched, scared and excited. Patsy picked as many as she could carry in her skirt – then we heard it, a man's voice and a barking dog. Patsy ran as fast as she could towards the fence.

"Run!" she yelled.

An old man came running towards Patsy, shaking a big stick, with his dog jumping and barking next to him, looking excited at the prospect of biting someone. I felt stuck to the spot. "Run," she yelled again, and I started to run as Patsy scrambled back over the fence, apples tumbling from her skirt. We kept on running. Patsy laughed all the way as I struggled to keep up.

"Thieving, dirty evacuees," the man yelled, but he didn't follow us.

When we were out of the sound of the barking dog and yelling man, we stopped and Patsy offered me an apple. I held my hands behind my back.

"What's wrong?" asked Patsy. "Here, take it."

"Sister Theresa said we mustn't steal, it's a mortal sin." I had no idea what "mortal sin" meant, but when any of the nuns said it, they shook their finger at us or banged their desk with their sticks. I imagined "mortal sin" must be like "blackout."

"Sister Tractor? Don't be silly," Patsy told me, "there are plenty of apples on the ground going to waste. He's just a mean old man, and besides, it's not stealing – it's scrumping."

The nuns never said anything about scrumping. So, I opened my mouth wide and bit down hard. Juice dribbled down my chin as I gobbled it up, core and all.

"Sister Tractor?" I asked.

"That's what we call her," said Patsy. "Have you seen the size of her feet?" I hadn't, but thinking of the grumpy nun as Sister Tractor made me laugh.

Before we came here, Patsy had barely noticed me, but now she talked to me, told me stories, shared her apples. Held my hand.

★　★　★

Every night, I lay in bed waiting to hear Patsy's soft, steady breathing. That's when I knew she was truly asleep and I climbed over her to the outside of the bed, away from the dark wall. I held my tiny doll and whispered important things that happened that day, like the yummy apple, to Ted.

CHAPTER 7

CHANGE

*And by and by Christopher Robin came to an end of things, and
he was silent, and he sat there, looking out over the world, just
wishing it wouldn't stop.* A.A. Milne

Sirens screamed. I jumped out of bed. Patsy grabbed me. She wrapped
her arms around me and said, "Shush." The sound was loud and a
sharp pain stabbed my ears. My body shook all over. I held tight to Patsy
so I wouldn't run away. That's what I felt like doing – running as fast as I
could, across the open field, far enough to get away from the noise. The
sirens went on forever, moaning and screaming, up and down. Patsy held
me until the all-clear sounded – a flat, dead groan.

"There, Pet," she said. "It's all over now, go to sleep." I couldn't let her
go, but she didn't push me away. She hugged me all night long.

That's when I started biting my nails. I was too big to suck my thumb,
Patsy told me, but no one said anything about biting nails. Patsy never bit
hers.

★　★　★

Somehow, I got through that first week without my Ted, and on the Saturday, Mrs. Croft gave Patsy money to take me to the morning pictures. It was the very first time I went to the pictures, though I knew what they were from Patsy talking with her friends. Patsy picked seats three rows from the front, where the screen dropped down to the stage floor. It was going to be a funny Mickey Mouse cartoon, Patsy said, and I slid down in my seat so I could see the whole screen. I already knew about Mickey Mouse. Besides, my gas mask was named Mickey Mouse and was supposed to look like him.

The picture started. Everything looked so large that I was gobbled up inside the film. Happy music played: the sky was deep blue with round, white clouds, and there was Mickey, whistling as he walked down a busy street. Just what I expected of Mickey, happy and having fun. I snuggled deeper into my seat.

Then Mickey accidentally knocked over a fruit stand. The fruit man yelled, frightening Mickey. He ran, and the man chased him – into the bakery, into the butcher shop. I bolted upright in my seat.

"Run Mickey, run," I yelled. And poor Mickey, running for his life, knocked over all the bread, all the cakes, all the sausages. Food flew everywhere, around and behind him. It wasn't his fault, but the butcher with his huge knife in his fat hand, the baker with his big wooden rolling pin, and all the people hit by the flying food joined in the chase, shaking their fists and yelling.

"They're going to kill Mickey Mouse," I screamed. I looked around. Why was everyone laughing? It wasn't funny. The baker with his rolling pin, the butcher with his big knife – didn't anyone see how dangerous it was for Mickey!

I yelled some more, but they wouldn't listen – they just kept on laughing. I turned around and knelt on my seat and yelled louder, "They're killing Mickey!"

Patsy dragged me, screaming, from the cinema.

"You embarrassed me no end," she scolded, "I'm not bringing you anymore."

I promised I'd be good, and every Saturday I kept that promise by burying my face in my hands whenever bad things happened.

My favourite pictures were musicals about Canadian Mounties and their beautiful horses, with Nelson Eddy and Jeanette MacDonald singing in forests and by glassy lakes. (That's when all the boys booed). The songs were happy, except for one when the mountains separated them: "I'll be calling you…oo oo ooo oo oo ooo/ Will you answer too…oo oo oooo oo oo ooo." But even then, I knew the ending would be happy. I really admired Jeanette MacDonald. She was so pretty and bright and never frightened of anything.

After the cartoons and before the picture, the news came on. The news was in black-and-white and the newsman sounded like a teacher as he told us how many people died that day and the terrible things that were happening, somewhere. Grey ships sailed on grey water – the greyness broken by the ships' white wake and black smoke from their guns – grey fires burned buildings until they crumbled, black airplanes flew in a grey endless sky, and the war seemed unreal, like the pictures.

Newsreels were loud and boring. Everyone thought so. The boys made war with spit balls and stood up to throw them around, which ended when the lights were turned on and a grown-up paced the aisles looking for the guilty.

The boys had just started playing war when the air-raid siren screamed. The picture was shut off, and all around me was black darkness. Boys yelled and whistled and stamped their feet. Grown-ups with big torches walked along the aisles, piercing the pitch-black space with wide beams of light, shouting over the din, telling us to go to the nearest shelter. They waved their torches around, making sure no one was hiding under the seats, moving, dizzying sweeps of light. What a nuisance! Everyone groaned about if they would get their money back. Now what would we do with our day? And I was confused with all the noise and being pushed about in the dark by the big boys. They grumbled the most.

Reluctantly, we left, dawdling and grumbling, carrying our cardboard-boxed gas masks while the grown-ups with torches yelled, "Hurry along now," and "Go to the nearest shelter," which I remember doing only once. It was dark inside and smelled just awful, like a lavatory, and I refused to stay. Patsy didn't want to, either.

Every Saturday we went to the pictures. It was the best part of the week. On this day, the picture was in colour and I watched the lady's long pink dress swirl around her as she danced, she was so beautiful, so sparkly. I pretended she was me. Patsy grabbed my arm, said our name was on the screen. "Look," she said, "there's a message, right there, at the bottom of the film, Daddy's outside." I saw the scratched message, white on black, I could read our names, "Patsy and Joan Kelleher."

"How do they do the writing, Patsy?"

"Hurry up," Patsy said as she ran, dragging me from the cinema. I kept my eyes on the screen. "I don't want to leave," I yelled. Patsy pulled me harder, told me I was being a brat, that Daddy was waiting. But I didn't care. I didn't care if I saw my father or not. Besides, it was a lovely picture, and we would miss it. Outside a soldier waited with his trouser legs tucked into his boots *That must be him*, I thought.

"Hello, Dizzy," he said, and picked up Patsy and twirled her around and around. I stood and watched and waited for my turn, which didn't come.

"I'm going away for a while," he said. "Came to say goodbye." Patsy said she didn't want him to go away, that she missed him. I missed Mummy, but I didn't miss *him*.

We sat on a wooden bench with splinters, and he told Patsy about the village where he was staying, about the cow he saw in a tree. Everyone knows cows don't go in trees, birds go in trees, maybe a cat, like Mrs. Cooper's old tabby, but cows are just too big and I told him so. He said this cow was thrown in the tree by a bomb. And everyone knows bombs don't throw things around, they squash everything flat.

I started to tell him that too, but he took hold of Patsy's hand and said, "Let's go for a little walk." I followed close beside Patsy and listened to the loud clunk of my father's big boots.

★ ★ ★

Sometimes we walked through the housing estate on our way home. Boys played marbles and conkers with horse chestnuts dangling from strings, and girls skipped rope and played hopscotch. I watched them play, wanting to join in, never brave enough to ask. Patsy got impatient with me one day. Told me to find my own way home. I barely heard her. I was holding my favourite marble up to the sky, turning it around in my fingers, completely absorbed in its lovely, smooth shape, wondering how the dark-green spiral got inside. I had all my pretty marbles with me that day; each one of them with different coloured shapes inside and collected from muddy gutters.

At the corner of our lane, there they were, about six boys yelling and playing a game of marbles. Their knees were scabby, and their short, dirty hair spiked out of their heads. The biggest boy with spiked-up hair stood in front of me, blocking my way. His narrow eyes glared at me. My legs tingled with fear, until he asked to look at my marble. I pulled all of them out of my pocket, only too pleased to show off.

"Want to play?" he asked.

Suspicious of this invitation, I took a step back. Boys usually avoided girls, especially babies like me. I was more than four, less than five.

"Come on," he said, "I'll show you." He held out his dirty hand and I saw the biggest marble ever, there was a chip in it, but the colours twisting around inside were beautiful. "I promise to play fair." I wanted that marble.

So, kneeling in the pebbly gutter, I played the way he showed me, flicking the marble with my bitten-down thumbnail. With his friends cheering me on, it seemed I won. I bent down, greedily looking at my treasure of marbles, ready to pick it up, but in the blink of an eye, two big fists whisked it all away.

"Cheater, cheater," his friends teased as he shoved the marbles into his pockets.

"You lost fair and square, to a girl," the boy with red hair said, dragging out "girl."

It didn't make any difference to him. He turned to leave in angry silence. Just like the Easter egg man, I thought. I grabbed his jumper and held fast.

"Give me my marbles," I said. He shook me off like a dog would a fly, and I fell to the pavement. He laughed at me, which made my face burn and ears ring.

"I'm going to tell my big sister." And scrambling to my feet, I ran to get Patsy. She could fix anything. *"I'm going to tell my big sister,"* he said in a baby voice and laughed some more.

As fast as I could, I ran towards the cottage, yelling for Patsy. And along the lane she came, running towards the big bully, yelling, "Give my little sister back her marbles!"

Hands in pockets, he just kept walking away from her. Patsy put two fingers in her mouth, whistled as loud as she could and dashed in front of him. Placing her hands on his shoulders, she gave him her scary stare. Standing still, feet planted in place, he asked, "Wha' yer goin' do. Make me?"

"Yes!" Patsy reached for the hand holding the marbles, now wedged in his pocket.

"Right!" he said, clenched his other fist and punched her in the face.

Patsy put her hands to her mouth. Bright red blood streamed through her fingers. I screamed, and Patsy kicked the grinning boy, first with one foot then the other, each kick came with a word: "You…bloody…cowardly…bully." Her final kick met air as he ran off laughing, with all my precious marbles.

Patsy lost a front tooth that day. She didn't cry. But I did. I sobbed all the way back to the cottage for Patsy's lost tooth.

Mrs. Croft told us to stay away from the housing estate. "The roughies live there," she said, as she placed a wet rag on Patsy's puffy mouth.

Poor Patsy, there was a hole in her mouth where her tooth used to be. I couldn't finish my tea. How I longed for Ted. Patsy said to follow her, she would teach me how to play "cat's cradle." We sat on our bed, and four hands hopelessly entwined in lengths of wool became one. Patsy teased and laughed when I tried to take the cradle without dropping the threads, "Silly sausage," she said. I saw the black space where her tooth should be, heard the high whistle when she said "s" words. My tears fell. "Silly," she said, "it doesn't hurt." Whistle, whistle.

When I went to bed that night, I told Ted that I had lost my pretty marbles and Patsy had lost her tooth and how she whistled.

★　★　★

Every Friday, Mrs. Croft sat me on her lap in front of the fire and told me real fairy stories. The red-orange flames mesmerised me. I stared hard, looking for the blue in the white flame, and the words of the story came to life. I loved the feel of her comfy lap and the warmth of the fire. If Ted were sitting on my lap it would be perfect.

Just when I thought it couldn't be any nicer, Mrs. Croft told us Mother was coming to see us. Mummy was coming. We were going home!

Mummy arrived on Saturday – our picture day. I ran to the door to meet her. She was quiet and serious, and said, "Hello girls, how are you?" but didn't wait for an answer. There were no kisses either. She wanted to talk with Mrs. Croft. While disappointed, I cheered up when Mrs. Croft fixed Patsy and me jam sandwiches for our lunch, wrapped them in newspaper and gave us money to go to the pictures. Kisses could wait.

Mummy had left by the time we got back. I ran to the kitchen, the garden, but she wasn't there. She hadn't come to take us home. I didn't get to tell her about Ted. Did she notice Patsy's missing tooth?

"Come here, dearie," Mrs. Croft said, and lifted me on her lap; Patsy stood next to the fire. Mrs. Croft told me we were leaving her, that we were "placed elsewhere." Placed elsewhere. What does that mean? I stared. "Moved to another house," she told me.

"Why?"

"Your mother knows best, dearie."

I wiggled away from Mrs. Croft and grabbed Patsy's skirt. "Why?" I asked.

Patsy told me not to make a fuss, took hold of my hand and we sat on our bed. Then she whispered about Mummy not being pleased with our food, the dirty cottage, the outside toilet, or our tiny bed squeezed in the cupboard under the stairs. Especially the food. "Mummy told me she paid Mrs. Croft herself, and she gets the government allowance."

"But I *like* bread and jam," I told her. "I don't want to leave. I like it here."

"It will be all right, Pet, you'll see."

My skin prickled. I felt sick. Now I would never find Ted and he wouldn't be able to find me.

★   ★   ★

Mrs. Croft packed our suitcases. She folded and smoothed our clothes and patted them in the cases with a sigh. I watched her, but this time Ted wasn't in front of me and I felt afraid, like when the sirens sound or when the nuns shake their canes.

Strangers knocked at the door. Two brown-shoed ladies, one tall one short. They asked for Patsy. Gas mask in its cardboard box around my neck, pushing my packed suitcase in front of me with my leg, I followed her.

"Not you dear," the tall, skinny stranger told me. "Someone else will come for you." I looked at Patsy, she was kissing Mrs. Croft goodbye.

I asked Patsy, "*Why?*" She shrugged her shoulders. I looked at Mrs. Croft, but she wouldn't look at me. She stood by the table, twisting a corner of her apron between her fingers.

There must be a mistake.

I asked the strangers, "*Why?*"

Nobody explained, but someone mumbled that Patsy was "going up North." My mind froze, my head burned, my throat ached. I didn't cry. Couldn't cry.

I watched the car drive off. Patsy waved. I couldn't move.

Mrs. Croft told me it was very important not to make a fuss. That the grown-ups knew best. I should just "come along now" and "be a good girl."

"You don't want your new family to think you're a bad girl, do you, dearie?"

I held my little doll tight in my hand and sat dry-eyed on my suitcase by the door until two brown-shoed ladies came for me. Mrs. Croft kissed my cheek and said goodbye, but I refused to say goodbye to her or Mr. Croft.

Saying goodbye would make it real.

CHAPTER 8

SUFFER LITTLE CHILDREN

"When stuck in the river, it is best to dive and swim to the bank yourself before someone drops a large stone on your chest in an attempt to whoosh you there." Eeyore, A.A. Milne

It was a big house, cold and dark and on the other side of town. A thin red line of lipstick cut across the mother's face, her hair was short and frizzy. Her narrow eyes stared at me as if I was not there and her lips were pulled in tight as if they did not know how to smile. Her hands moved down the front of her apron, smoothing it as if wiping something nasty away. Two children almost as big as Patsy stood next to her. The girl's long plaits were tied with pink ribbons and the boy picked at the spots on his face.

They did not want me – I could tell – there were no smiles, nobody said "hello," they just stood and glared, the three of them – the mother, the son, the daughter.

What were their names? The stranger said them so fast, then left me in the hallway with my ration books, my suitcase, my gas mask. My stomach tightened harder, like when the air raids screamed. My legs shook.

"Father, look what the cat drug in." With her hand on the back of my head, the mother pushed me into the living room, where the father was sitting in front of a fire, reading the paper. "Name's Kelleher, an Irish brat, is this one. Catholic too." He just sat there and didn't look at me.

"Humph," she said. "As if I don't have enough on my hands. Now this! Bloody war."

The father rustled his paper and coughed, but still didn't look. How I missed Patsy. She knew so much about grown-ups and would know what to say to this family and get them to say "hello."

"You're not to come in here," she said, pointing to the living room. There were flowers in the middle of the table. I couldn't see the vase, just the tops of pretty flowers. We walked to the kitchen, where I would eat my meals, wash my face, my knickers and my socks, and to the outside toilet, which I would use. The toilet door was in the garden, though part of the house, not separate like Mrs. Croft's. Three round holes cut in the top of the wooden door let in the only light. Trickles of water slid in slow streams down the painted bricks to the cement floor, covered in a grey-green fuzz. It smelled awful, like the air-raid shelter near the pictures.

I followed the mother upstairs to a room, which would be mine. It was full of boxes and suitcases. The ceiling sloped, like the cupboard under the stairs. A tiny-eyed window faced the door and a narrow bed stood along one wall, its top facing the window.

"You'll speak only when spoken to in this house and take care of yourself. This is your room. You stay in here and behave." She started to leave, then noticed my shoelace was undone.

"Tie that shoe."

"I can't."

"No such word as 'can't,'" she said, and with a sigh told me to sit on the bed, and demonstrated, "Right over left, pull it under, make a loop, wrap it around and pull it through, then make the bow, like this." She untied them and left me to practice.

My legs dangled down. I stared at them. What is right and left? It seemed my hands were on backwards and my fingers wouldn't work. But somehow, I managed to tie a knot and half a bow. Mrs. Croft had tied my laces before. "There, dearie," she would say, "you won't trip over those."

I lay on the cold bed with all my clothes on, shoes too, and stared into the dark, ready to run, waiting for one of the boxes to move or open up to let out the creatures that live in the dark. I crawled under the blanket. If I held it up around my nose maybe *it* wouldn't find me. The more I stared, the lighter the room became. The square boxes became bigger as they moved closer to my bed. I tried but couldn't stop staring.

Straining my ears, I heard nothing.

I thought of the cozy cupboard under the stairs, the light from the fire shining on the walls, and Mrs. Croft's smile, Mr. Croft's Victory Garden. How I missed Patsy. How I missed Ted. He knew I didn't like the dark. I tried to pretend he was with me. I whispered his name, "Ted, Ted," but he hadn't seen this house and so I could not see him. I wondered where Patsy was, though I knew my big sister could take care of grown-ups, bullies too.

Birds were singing. It was morning.

"Hurry up," yelled the mother, and I heard the boy and girl run down the stairs. I went to the kitchen, where cold lumpy porridge waited for me. There was no sugar or milk, but I was very hungry and swallowed it down. I felt a hard lump in my throat, so I drank the cold, milky water quickly to keep the porridge from coming back up.

There were spiders in the lavatory! Running into the corners, among the fuzz, when I opened the door, and up the walls. Long legs and round, fat bodies, and I knew they had teeth; big teeth ready to nip me.

Holding my breath against the stink, I sat on the cold, wooden seat. I couldn't reach the chain to flush. With hands on the slimy wall, I climbed up onto the toilet seat, stretched out my arm as the chain swung away from me.

"Get down from there!" yelled the foster mother, making me jump so high I almost fell in.

"Here, take this bucket," she said, handing me the rusty handle. "Fill it up, then pour it in the bowl, until it flushes." It took many trips to the garden tap to get enough water.

Every time I went to the spider-lavatory, I kept my eyes moving to make sure I didn't squash one or it didn't bite me. (It was a sin to squash spiders; they had saved Jesus and Mary from the soldiers. Sister Theresa had told us so.) It's difficult looking around when sitting on a toilet, holding on with your hands because your feet are nowhere near touching the ground. And it was dark in there, even in the daytime, but I still closed the door so nobody saw me. By nighttime it was pitch-black, mornings too, and I imagined long-legged spiders crawling around, watching, waiting.

★ ★ ★

Two nuns stood at the door, waiting to take me to school. They stood in the open doorway, blocking the light. I looked at their faces, hoping to see a smile. The only part that showed was the middle: their eyes, hiding behind glasses and their tight-lipped mouths, the rest hidden by white, shiny cloth that looked as thick as metal. They did not look at my face and I wondered how they knew it was me. "Hurry along now," were their only words, spoken in tight voices. Their clothes smelled like mothballs and took up so much space I couldn't see anything but straight in front, and then they walked so fast I couldn't see in front either as I almost ran to keep up. I waited for one to look at me to see if I was still there, but with heads in the air, hands clasped inside their wide sleeves, they floated along, the only living part of them their black rosary beads, which hung from their belted waists and swung with each step. They came every day until I knew the way. Sundays, they were always there to take me to Mass. The mother never invited them in.

We walked for a long time, but not to Saint Anne's. We arrived at a big school, "The Salesian Boys School," they told me. Huge trees and mowed lawns surrounded the buildings. Two small hills sat alongside, with sandbags at each doorway. They were shelters, Anderson shelters; this family had one in their garden.

I followed the nuns into a classroom. It was very quiet. I could hear my feet on the wooden floor. Windows stood open at the top of the high wall, but it was still dark inside. Girls sat close together and I walked to the front of the room, as told, and sat at a desk with another girl. A red-faced nun, stick in hand, peered at me over the top of shiny glasses. "Name?" she asked. I whispered my name. Her name was Sister Ann.

The girl next to me turned her head towards me. "Stop that fidgeting," Sister Ann said, and beat our desk with her stick. My heart jumped.

We had little blackboards at this school and pieces of chalk to write with. The chalk was thick and round, flat on the top. Sister Ann pointed to the letters on the big blackboard and outlined their shape with her stick. We were to copy the letters onto our boards, and tongue between my teeth,

I set to it. The room filled with the squeaky sounds of dry chalk. Soon my board was covered in shaky lines, that's when we had to wipe them clean with our hands.

★ ★ ★

Sister Ann held up a Holy Picture of Jesus, sitting on a chair in Heaven, with angels around him in the blue sky and children in long white gowns climbing onto his lap. (Every time we said Jesus, we had to bow our heads, making His name sound longer, Jeee-SUS.) There was gold writing at the bottom.

"Jesus is saying, 'Suffer little children to come unto me,'" she said. I wondered what that meant. I knew Jesus wouldn't want children hurt in order to live with Him in Heaven. He was kind and gentle and listened to my prayers.

There was a picture of Jesus on the wall behind Sister Ann. There were thorns on His head and blood dripped down. I could see His heart, with flames coming out of it, red and orange flames out of His red heart. I wondered if it hurt, but He wasn't crying. Poor Jesus. He did that for all of us, Sister Ann said, except for the babies in darkest Africa. They were in Limbo because their parents didn't know about Him and they couldn't be saved. Not ever, not even at the end of the world. They weren't Catholics. My mother wasn't Catholic, what would happen to her?

Sister Ann liked to blow her whistle, she liked to beat desks too so you had to pay attention, and the blackboard got a real thrashing. The best girl of the day got to clean the blackboard and bang the erasers together and make chalk clouds. I wanted that job, but all the chosen girls had ribbons in their hair and smiled with little round white teeth.

The same nuns were waiting for me and walked me back to the cold house and rang the bell. They walked faster on the way back, and after the mother opened the door they turned and left without saying a word.

"Tea's on the table," she said. "Eat up."

Two thick slices of fluffy bread waited on a plate. I watched the mother shake milk powder into a cup of water and jumped when she slammed it in front of me. I wondered where the jam was. Where the cod-liver oil and orange juice were that would make me big and strong. I looked up at her.

"What are you looking at?" she asked. I didn't know how to answer and kept staring. "Insolent, that's what you are, my girl," she said, and hit the side of my head hard. I grabbed the table as my chair fell to the floor. My ears rang. I was too frightened to cry.

It was hard to swallow the bread.

★ ★ ★

Once I knew the way to and from school, I went on my own. When the nuns took me, I'd had to "hurry along," so I'd not had time to notice the fields. Brown and white cows and beautiful horses stood under trees with nothing to do except flick at flies and nibble at grass. I kept my eyes on them as I walked, longing to touch them, longing to feel the horses' velvet noses, like Fred's horse Rhubarb's when he nibbled the carrot I gave him.

There were no shelters for the cows or horses. The cows looked as if they didn't care; they were always busy chewing and occasionally lifted their heads to give me a sleepy gaze before going back to their grass. Horses were different; they really looked at me, with eyes that were bright and friendly, and their ears stood up as if they were trying to hear what I might be saying.

Just as I was picking my bread-and-cheese leaves to ease the hunger pains, a horse walked up to the hedge. He blew through his wide, wet nostrils and little drops of water sprinkled out on his face. "Hello," I said. His huge brown eyes looked right at me and I thought he wrinkled his forehead. "You're beautiful," I told him. He shook his head and walked slowly away. I watched as he gently scattered the grass with his breath, looking for the tender shoots. I watched the grass move and I saw tiny daisies and buttercups, hiding.

I ran to the railing, climbed up and peered over the hedge to see the horses better, a fistful of grass in my hand. "Here horse, horse," I called. The big brown one with the white face walked towards me again and wriggled his nose and blew clouds of white, sweet-smelling steam in the air. He sniffed at the tops of the grass clenched in my fist. I felt his warm breath, his velvet nose soft as the collar on my best blue coat as he nibbled the grass. "I'm Joanie, and you're my new friend," I told him and watched his ears move back and forth while I spoke, and laughed when he swished his tail and shook his head in agreement.

Horses really noticed me, unlike the grown-ups whose eyes did not want to look at mine.

I must have stayed with the horses for a long time; it was very quiet at school when I finally arrived. I walked to the door of my classroom and opened it, slowly. Sister Ann stared at me through her thick glasses, the whole class stared at me and I stood still, too frightened to move.

"Sit," she said, hitting my desk with her cane. "I'll deal with you later."

I sat and waited for later, wishing it was now. Break time came, that was the "later." Sister Ann said I could not go out for any breaks today, that I had to "sit and contemplate my evil ways."

I didn't know what "contemplate" meant, but thought it might mean to think, so I thought about the beautiful horses, their beautiful friendly eyes, their soft noses, and my heart smiled. "Contemplate" was wonderful.

The bell rang twice, home time. Sister Ann stood by my desk. "If you're late again, there will be more serious consequences," she said. I looked at the cane and decided to pick grass for my friends on the way back to the house instead of the mornings.

I took my little doll from her hiding place under the mattress and told her about the horses. "I saw the big brown one with the soft white nose today, he's my favourite." She fit in the palm of my hand, and I clenched her tight while I slept. She didn't keep me warm like Ted had, or Patsy. But it felt good to have her to hold on to.

Saturday came. It was washday in this house. Mother had said, "One to wear, one for spare, one in the wash." The "spare" had gone missing. So I put on my clean pair of socks and knickers and set off for the kitchen. I remembered seeing Mummy rub soap on wet clothes, so I climbed up on a chair, tried to grab the huge bar of slippery green soap and turned on the tap. It spluttered and spat. The soap fell. Icy water hit my chest. I gasped. Water splashed on the draining board, my toes, the chair, the floor.

Goosebumps crawled over my skin. Before I could turn off the tap, slaps smarted the back of my legs, one, two, three. I grabbed the sink as I fell and bit my lip to keep from crying.

"Wipe it up," my foster mother told me, "all of it," and threw a rag on the floor. My hands shook as I wiped up the mess. I kept my eyes lowered so she wouldn't say I was "insolent." "Insolent" meant a slap on the head, which made my ears ring, and I didn't know when I might do it.

The mother filled a bowl with water and gave me a wooden board with metal ridges on it. "Scrub them on this," she said, and I scrubbed. I scrubbed away the dirt from my socks and all the skin from my knuckles.

★ ★ ★

The boy and girl were usually in the living room sitting by the fire when I came in from school, the door open just a crack. I crept past them into the kitchen. We had silently agreed to ignore each other. The Monday after the washing day, they were sitting on the stairs, waiting. I kept my eyes on the floor and didn't look at them, hoping they wouldn't notice me.

"Charge," the boy yelled, and I flattened myself against the wall as they ran past me, hands extended, planes in flight, shooting at me, yelling, "got you, you bloody Jerry." I almost yelled in fear, but then I would get a "what for" and they knew it. I didn't like them one bit, and wished I were brave like Patsy. Back in my room, I thought how I'd kick them and trip them up next time. I'd pull the girl's hair too, until she cried. I'd catch spiders and put them in the girl's bed, maybe the boy's too, though he'd probably squash them.

Whenever their father wasn't there, they played that trick on me. I never knew when that would happen, which made it extra scary when it did.

★ ★ ★

My foster mother told me my mother was coming, that I had to behave and look my best. My heart thumped in my ears. *Mummy is coming. She's coming to move me. She must know that there's no jam here, only bread and lumpy porridge.* Though there were potatoes and cabbage on Sunday, but no carrots, no yummy orange juice. *She is certain to move me.* Perhaps I could go back and live with Mr. and Mrs. Croft and sleep in the cupboard under the stairs. Perhaps I could live with Patsy "up North." I wanted to jump with excitement but could not let the mother know of these happy thoughts.

"Put on clean clothes and wash that filthy face," my foster mother said.

I climbed up to the kitchen sink and splashed cold water on my face, then rushed to my room, out of her way. Clean clothes waited on my bed – and a gymslip, my first. All the other girls wore them. I pulled my jumper over my head, buttoned up a new white blouse and inspected my navy-blue gymslip. It smelled clean, fresh. There were two buttons on each shoulder. I stepped into it, held it up with my elbows and reached back for the button-holes. Every time I got hold of the back, I lost the front. Perhaps my arms were too short. I used my chin to hold up the front, but it still kept slipping down. My fingers began to shake.

Frustrated and frightened that I wouldn't be dressed in time to see my mother, I forgot the "no crying, or making a fuss" rule.

The door crashed open, her face red as fire, scrunched into tight lines, her eyes dark bars, she lurched at me. Something warm trickled down my legs.

Grabbing my shoulders, she shook me, her fingers digging into my bones, screaming over and over, "Be quiet!" and if I told my mother any-thing, I'd get a "what for."

I couldn't breathe, my teeth were breaking, my neck was breaking, the floor was gone. I opened my eyes wide and stared at her face. If she saw my eyes open, she would know I wasn't crying – wouldn't she? She let me go. I fell to the floor.

Dragging me into a bathroom, which I hadn't seen before, she scrubbed my face and neck, tugged at the tangles in my hair with a comb, handed me the washcloth and told me to clean myself off.

"Here, put these on," she said and threw me a pair of the girl's knickers.

★ ★ ★

Mummy arrived and was greeted with, "Hello, nice to meet you," by the mother. They exchanged smiles and shook hands. I stood in the passage and waited for Mummy to notice me.

"This way, Mrs. Kelleher," and Mummy went in the sitting room. A fire burned in the hearth. "Sit here, you must be cold." Mummy sat in one of the two armchairs and removed her leather gloves, one finger at a time, smoothed them on her lap and placed them on top of her handbag. The foster mother smiled and asked in a soft singsong, "How was the journey, Mrs. Kelleher?"

"Quite fast, actually, less than an hour, even with changes. Crowded, but I did get a seat."

I tiptoed inside the door and watched the two smiling women as they continued to chat like friends, about rationing, "dreadful," the shortage of clothing, "shameful." The more I listened, the further away they sounded, until I wasn't there at all.

"Joan. Joan, don't stand there, dear, come and sit on this chair," instructed the mother, and patted one of the dining chairs arranged by the fire. I carefully climbed up and Mummy looked at me, gave me a smile. She was so beautiful. My mouth opened, but before I could speak, I heard, "Here, Mrs. Kelleher, a nice cup of tea, do you want sugar?"

"Gave it up, rationing you know."

They laughed

The foster mother gave me a cup of fresh milk. It was delicious. The first cup of milk I'd had in this house. Then she handed me dainty sandwiches and biscuits on a flowery plate. The biscuits were decorated with white and pink icing. Not even Mrs. Croft had biscuits. I wasn't sure if I should eat, or just hold the plate, until she said, "Your little girl is so shy. Eat up now, Joan."

Mummy remarked that I looked thin, "pale and thin." She said it with a worried face. I turned quickly to look at the foster mother, hoping her face would turn red.

"She's just going through a growing spurt; you know how that is," she said calmly, and passed the plate of fairy cakes. Mummy nodded.

There was no chance for me to speak, and I knew she wouldn't believe me now anyway. (It seemed that grown-ups always stuck together.) So I had to keep quiet and pretend. My heart pounded. I stared at my mother, silently pleading for her to notice something, anything, she didn't like about this family.

It was time to leave, and with a kiss on my forehead Mummy told me, "Be a good girl, now. Do what you're told." She was so close I could smell roses and home. I wanted to hold her coat, beg her to take me away. But I could feel the foster mother staring at me. I was too terrified to speak, to cry.

"Thank you for taking such good care of Joan," Mummy said. The sandwich turned to a solid lump in my throat. I watched her walk out the door.

"Come back, Mummy. Talk to me, hold me." I wanted to yell the words, but she was gone. I ran up the stairs to my room and sat on the floor by the window. My head hurt, a stabbing pain that cut my head in two.

CHAPTER 9

THE BATTLE OF BRITAIN

"It's snowing still," said Eeyore gloomily.
"So it is."
"And freezing."
"Is it?"
"Yes," said Eeyore, "however," he said, brightening up a little, "we
haven't had an earthquake lately." A.A. Milne

My room seemed extra cold and dark. My stomach hurt; a sharp pain that made me fold in half. A strip of light shone under my door. The family was up, sitting together in the warm, eating fried onions, boiled cabbage. I could smell it, and my stomach grumbled. I wondered if they had sausages too, fat, juicy sausages.

I sat on the bed, wishing I'd told Mummy I wanted to go away, far away from this family. She would take me if she knew, but she only saw the clean house, the warm fire, the treats on flowery china plates, the boy and girl that she thought were my friends.

Sirens screamed. They made my heart thump hard, but I was used to them now and didn't try to run away. I put my hands over my ears and turned my head to face the tiny-eyed window. Flashes of hot light sliced through the split in the curtains and exploded like thunder. I jumped up in bed, too frightened to scream. Sirens howled above the rat-tat-tat of guns and the sharp, shattering sound of airplanes fighting right outside my window. Noises vibrated through my frozen body like the boom from a big drum.

I squeezed up tight against the wall, held my knees to my chest, scrunched my eyes shut, dragged my blanket over my head, hiding from the flashing lights. I squirmed and became a prisoner of the tangled blanket as I tried to shake off the prickles chewing my skin. My heart thumped in my head. I held my breath, repeated my prayer, "Please God, please God" over and over, not knowing what I wanted to ask of God or even if I should bother him.

The all-clear moaned.

It was quiet, the night dark again. I stayed hidden in my blanket until the morning light shone through the crack in the curtain and the mother yelled, "hurry up."

I dressed and went to the kitchen to eat breakfast. Nobody spoke about the night noises. Perhaps they went to their shelter under the ground, and maybe it wasn't noisy there. I knew the bright lights wouldn't find them there.

On my way to school I saw girls huddled in circles, whispering. I wondered if they were talking about the night noises, but I didn't find out. Sister Ann didn't talk about the night noises either.

Night after night the air raids came. I sat in bed with all my clothes on, listening, waiting for the first sound of sirens winding up, saying the prayer I heard at school: "Gentle Jesus, meek and mild, Look upon a little child." That's all I could remember, and I repeated the words, over and over until I heard the family run down the stairs, the bang of the kitchen door as they went to their shelter in the garden. That's when I forgot all of the words. I crawled under the bed and hid among the balls of white dust. Sometimes my body froze and I couldn't move. And when the all-clear moaned, I stayed where I was, wide-eyed, waiting for the sirens to scream again.

Every day, after school, I ate my tea and then sat in my room, ears straining, jumping when a door banged, a floorboard squeaked. And every time I jumped, my heart beat faster, like a stutter. I waited for the air raids. I didn't change my clothes for bed. I didn't want to sleep. If I closed my eyes the planes might find me. I held my little doll and told her fairy stories about my family: "Once upon a time," they all began, and somehow, I was lost, but my mother always finds me and hugs me and takes me home. We sit by the fire and eat hot potatoes and carrots, buttered toast, sausages and onions, soft boiled eggs. Mummy smiles at me. I am never angry or upset at the wicked witch, or dragon, or beast that held me captive, just grateful for the aloneness to end.

I wrapped myself in my dreams, like a soft blanket, enjoying their safety and promise, unlike the air raids and nightmares over which I had no control.

★ ★ ★

After eating my breakfast bread, I picked my little doll from her hiding place under my mattress. The air raid seemed to have lasted all night and I was still shaking. My little doll would keep me company at school that day. My knickers were the best place for hiding her. I felt her bump against my leg as I walked. I thought up a name for her, Alice, that would be her name, it was a pretty name. It was good to have a friend.

Break time, and fat Sister Margaret showed us how to do jumping jacks in the asphalt yard. Some of the girls giggled, she did look funny with her clothes popping up and down, I even got to see her shoes. They were black and matched her thick stockings. Her face went red with effort and she said we were a "lazy lot."

I jumped like she showed us, and felt the elastic in my knickers leg break. Out fell my tiny doll to the ground. Sister Margaret walked towards me. Terror turned me cold. She called me a "deceitful child."

"Hold out your hands," she ordered, cane at the ready.

I didn't want to, but she pulled them forward, palms up. They wanted to get away from the cane, but I knew I must hold out my blue-red hands for the punishment for deceit. If not, there would be more. Down came the swishing cane – two whacks on my hands, and my doll was "confiscated," which I learned meant I could never have her back. Instead, I was left with two burning welts on my palms and a lecture about being dishonest. I didn't cry. Only crybabies cried.

Fingers raw and without my tiny doll to hold, I started chewing my toenails, ignoring the grit that scratched at my teeth. I made up stories about my mother who waited for me in our beautiful house with roses in the garden and in the crystal vase in the living room, and told them to Me.

★ ★ ★

I sat on a wooden chair in front of a scarred, ink-stained desk. Paper was too precious to waste on our class, so we used the air.

"Show me the capital letter A," Sister Ann asked, pointing to the letter on the blackboard. Her cane traced the lines, and hands in air, we drew the shape.

"Again," she said. We continued writing the alphabet until I thought my arm would fall off, though I had no idea if I was doing it properly. The only thing I did discover was that "klmop" is five letters and not one. When we had sung the Alphabet song, we'd always lumped them together.

There were no books, so as Sister Ann read, we repeated the language of prayer: "thy, thee, thou, womb, hallowed, trespass, Amen." She held up the book she was reading so we could see the pictures we weren't allowed to touch.

Part of prayer lessons was the Ten Commandments. We repeated them, one after the other, but Sister Ann didn't explain the meaning, leaving me confused and terrified of Hell and Sin. If you didn't know what Sin was, you could be doing it without knowing, and when you died, land up in Hell. "Thou shall not steal," I knew that one, but "Thou shall not commit adultery?" What is adultery? "Lusting," Sister Ann said. And what is lusting? And what about "Thou shall not kill?" What were the bombs doing? Though nobody spoke of the air raids, not even the nuns. "War" was the most confusing thing of all.

After break we repeated the times tables. I liked the sound, the rhythm: "two times two is four, three times two is six." With Sister Ann hitting the blackboard and pointing to the numbers it was almost like singing a song. Repeating the times tables was the only lesson that made any sense.

★ ★ ★

Air-raid sirens screeched. Sister Ann yelled, "Hold on to your gas masks and run, in an orderly fashion to the air-raid shelters." I ran towards the dugout in the earth, past the sandbags and down the stairs. It was dark, damp, scary inside. I felt the wet dirt walls, smelled the earth all around me, like a grave.

Boys joined us, and big girls from other classes. Pushing and shoving we sat on narrow wood planks along the walls. Wooden boards lay on the ground where nuns and men teachers, torches in hand, paced back and forth, puffed up and important. "Gas masks on," yelled a tall man.

I sat, trembling, trying to pull the rubber straps over my head. I couldn't breathe, the mask cut into my face, pulled my hair. I started to take it off.

"You there, what do you think you're doing?" He meant me, and I put my hands down.

"Repeat the times table for seven," the tall man said.

I heard the boys start, using silly voices, making fun of the teacher without him knowing. Though they said it differently, I joined in: "six sevens are forty two, seven sevens are forty nine..." It was fun, making silly voices, and soothing, repeating the numbers – that is until my eyeglass fogged up from my steamy breath. It seemed the air was being sucked out of me, closing down on my nose and mouth like a giant pillow.

The all-clear sounded, and we ran like wild things out of the shelter into the light, pulling off gas masks, gasping in air.

Sometimes we had practice air raids. It was good to get out of the classroom and sit close to the boys who were brave, like Patsy.

★　★　★

Boys were cheering. An army lorry had come to school to test our gas masks. We stood in lines, crocodile-style and the boys whispered, "Hold your breath, it's real gas." They laughed, but I believed them.

Seven or eight at a time, we were shoved into the lorry and sat on seats which faced inwards towards each other. It was my turn. Metal doors slammed closed and the handle clanked in place. It was dark inside. The single bulb barely illuminated my neighbors. The engine started, and there we were, sitting in the dark with the sound of the engine running, shaking my insides. I held my breath as long as I could, and when my lungs were ready to explode, gasped for air, not caring if I died. There was never enough. I gripped the metal seat tight with my hands, and my heart raced.

As soon as the doors opened, I was pushed outside along with the rest. I tore off the mask, along with trapped hair, sucked in the sweet-smelling air, my eyes blinking and watering in the daylight.

★   ★   ★

While you can squeeze your eyes shut, you can't squeeze your ears closed. I wanted to know what was happening outside at night, perhaps I would not be as frightened if I knew. That's what Patsy would say.

One night, when the flashes of light seemed far away and the noises not so loud, I tiptoed to the tiny-eyed window and peeked through the slit in the curtains. I stood still, holding my breath, and saw planes, big fat bombers and small fighters, disappearing in and out of wispy clouds, like giant birds, hunting.

The small, quick fighter planes fascinated me, especially when their gunfire lit up the sky, just like in the newsreels Patsy took me to. That's how I knew they were the fighters. I imagined the pilots as knights from fairy tales, fighting to free the beautiful princess from the evil witch, or dragon, or tower or something even more terrible that did not yet have a name.

Seeing what was happening freed up my mind from frozen fear, and I could think. Curiosity didn't kill the cat, in spite of what Patsy always said.

Later, I would learn to tell by the shapes of the planes and sounds of the engines which were "ours" and which were "theirs." Though I never did understand what "ours" and "theirs" really meant.

Air-raid warnings started slowly, softly, as if waking up. They became louder and louder, screeched higher and higher, and I'd strain my ears listening for the first sound of airplane engines. Sometimes it was a "false alarm" – that's what they called it if the planes didn't come. But when they did, I'd hear the mother whisper, "Hurry," then running footsteps down the stairs and the bang of the kitchen door as they rushed to their shelter. The bang made me jump, like a slap for being "insolent."

Inside, the house was very quiet. Quiet and hollow and empty. So empty that the walls seemed to disappear and I felt like I was sitting on a bed in the dark sky, the only person left in the world.

On nights I felt brave, I crawled to the window and peeped through the curtains. I listened to the sounds and stared as the night sky lit up with spurts of fire – the noise and fire going on at once, in slow motion it seemed: the beautiful dark night sky with its bright stars, the hot white, orange and red flames from the guns which blotted out the stars, the sky, and the piercing sounds of sirens and planes. These sights and sounds created a space of wonder in my mind, which I wanted to turn into questions, but for some questions I knew there were no answers and so they never formed.

After a night of bombing there was always a strange silence in the morning; the birds didn't sing. As the day went on, they started, with just one or two at first, but it seemed to take them a whole day to sing again. I really missed hearing them. Everywhere seemed emptier.

Were they frightened or sad?

★ ★ ★

The head nun came into our classroom. We all stood up. Sister Ann called the nun "Mother." "Mother" was very tall, thin too. Her voice was soft, the kind of soft that makes everyone listen. She asked for the guilty person to "come forward," the one who had written a forbidden word on the wall outside her office. "If you do, your classmates will be spared," she said. "Spared?" What did that mean? I think we were all confused because nobody "came forward."

"Line up at eleven, Sister," she said, then left.

Sister Ann gave us a lecture on dishonesty, which I'd heard before, then about thinking of others and not yourself and things I just didn't understand. We then said ten Hail Marys.

"Form a line, single file," Sister Ann said, and led us out of our room towards the office.

There was already a line of girls standing there, big girls. We were the last. Whispers echoed around, girls with red faces walked past us, some of them crying. A piece of dried-up orange peel was passed to me. "Rub it on your hand, it will take the sting away," the girl said. So, as I wondered about where the orange peel came from, I did as she said and passed it, along with the message, to the girl behind me.

There was the word, written in white chalk on the red brick wall. Such a small word to cause so much trouble. I hadn't seen it before and didn't know what it meant, and I couldn't read it anyway. Then it was my turn, and into the office I went.

"Hold out your hands, both of them," Mother said.

I knew what that meant and thought she must think I'm stupid to hold out my hands to be hit. I was given a choice – hold out my hands for three, or she would hold them for six. Shaking all over I held out my hands. On the last stroke I pulled them back. The cane bit into my bones, which hurt more than my hand. Why did they have to hit so hard? Why were they so angry? They should be kind. They talked about Jesus every day, all day, and Jesus loved everyone and wanted us to love each other. I put my burning hands gently under my arms, but I didn't cry.

★   ★   ★

On my way to school one morning, after a night of heavy bombing, I saw what I thought was a cow in a tree. Something was lying on the top branches. It looked like a cow. The more I stared the more it looked like a brown and white cow, skinny legs bent and floppy. My father was right! Cows do get blown into trees. There was nobody to ask, but I could tell it was dead. I felt sorry for the cow, but better a cow than a horse, and wondered if someone would get it down.

The tree was all right – trees lived for hundreds of years, Sister Ann told us so. I decided to plant a tree, an oak tree. I found an acorn in the grass by my feet and planted it in the very middle of a lovely green space where it would get lots of sun, and reflected with pleasure that long after I died, the tree would still be there.

The green space was the lawn in front of the school, mowed weekly. I gasped when I saw the tractor kill my tree. Week after week it died, again and again.

But I helped the worm. It was on a cold, wet morning, on the path that led to school that I saw him, a worm, trodden on and torn in two, each piece wriggling around in distress. Using my teeth, I tore a strip from my hankie, placed the two yellow, smashed ends of the wiggly pink worm onto the cloth, tied him carefully back together again and placed him between blades of grass so the birds wouldn't swoop down from the sky and kill him.

Days and nights passed, the only marker Mass on Sunday and yummy boiled potatoes and cabbage for dinner. Some nights I was a spectator standing at the tiny-eyed window, watching, spellbound by the awesome beauty in front of me. Some nights my legs wouldn't take me to the window, and I'd lay curled up under my bed, gripped in stomach churning, ice-cold fear, wishing the floorboards would open up and I could disappear, forever.

CHAPTER 10

WINTER

"Many happy returns of the day," said Piglet again.
"Meaning me?"
"Of course, Eeyore."
"My birthday?"
"Yes."
"Me having a real birthday?"
"Yes, Eeyore, and I've brought you a present." A.A. Milne

Indian summer didn't come that year. One day it was warm, the next cold. The days became short and dark. It was a bitter cold and the cold hurt, a burning pain, which stiffened my body and froze my face. At night, I covered my head with my blanket, wrapped my icy feet in my nightie, tried hard not to let them touch another part of me, as I curled into a ball. I closed my eyes and tried to feel Mrs. Croft's soft lap, her gentle hands around my middle, as Ted and I lazed in front of the warm fire and listened to her crackly voice tell me stories of princesses, palaces and Cinderella.

Winter mornings, though, were magical and almost made up for the cold. Trees sparkled with frozen dewdrops and pavements were white with frost, sometimes snow. I loved the snow, and on the first snowy day I twirled in the falling flakes, face up to the sky, dizzying spins of white, as though I was falling from Heaven down to earth. I opened my mouth, stuck out my tongue to see how many snowflakes I could catch without having to blink. Robins, as round and rosy as apples, hopped busily around, leaving crisscross patterns in the snow. Red holly berries peeked through the white. The only colours were black trees, white snow and little red spots. Everything dirty and grey whitened out. It looked like a fairyland. I tried not to step on the fresh snow and spoil it.

But the cold pavement soon stiffened my feet until I thought they would snap in two. I breathed on the blue-red tips of my fingers and held them under my arms. I longed to touch the radiator in our classroom, but we weren't allowed. I stood as close as I could and watched the steam float around me and smelled the sour smell of dirt and wet wool.

On the way back to the cold house, the lovely white snow had turned to brown sludge. It covered my shoes and sneaked through the cracks in the leather and turned my feet to ice.

Chilblains inflamed my hands and legs, my feet. Skin peeled back from the angry bumps and oozed yellow pus and my socks stuck to my feet as if glued. I shuffled along on the backs of my shoes, unlaced for extra room. But "at least you have shoes on your feet," said my foster mother, which was true enough. There were plenty of children without shoes at all, she told me, "Especially you Irish."

It hurt too much when I tried to take my socks off, so I went to bed with all my clothes on and pulled my nightie over the top.

No matter the weather, I stopped by the fields to visit the horses. Their breath came out like steam from a kettle and sometimes bounced off their backs. They shook snow off their thick winter coats, and their manes waved along their necks. They stood together, head to tail, looking after each other, keeping each other warm. My mouth was frozen shut, so I clicked my tongue at the brown one with the white nose. He came to me and I put my face right in front of his and he breathed on me and I felt his warmth, like a hug. I touched his soft cheek. His coat seemed thicker now. I was glad.

★ ★ ★

Sister gave us each a piece of precious paper. She said we could draw the Holy Family. Sister said it would be Jesus's birthday soon, a time to pray extra hard for peace. With stiff fingers, I tried to draw the baby Jesus.

I saw Him in church, a beautiful china baby with golden hair, lying on straw, smiling, his arms reaching out to me. China sheep breathed on him to keep him warm, and Mary and Joseph watched over him, praying. Mustn't complain, Sister told us. Jesus was poor and cold with nowhere to live. We must thank Him for all our blessings, and we would be rewarded, here, or in Heaven.

God bless Mummy, and thank you for my blessings. Amen.

★ ★ ★

It was my sixth birthday. I knew it was so, as the mother called me into the living room and gave me an envelope.

"Your birthday card," she said. They were all there, the parents and the two children. A fire was burning in the grate. I looked at the envelope. There were stamps on it. Someone knew where I was. Knew it was my birthday. I didn't even know it was my birthday. I stared at the mother.

"It's from your grandmother."

Feeling grateful to this person I didn't know, I carefully opened the envelope and pulled out a card. My very first card! It was small and delicate, made of celluloid, with gold lettering and embossed with the shapes of bluebirds. I ran my fingers over the birds and felt the shape of plump chests, feathery wings and tiny, thin legs. I could see the birds and close my eyes and feel them and see them again in my mind. It was the most beautiful thing I'd ever seen, more beautiful than any holy picture, and it belonged to me.

"Oh," I gasped, and held it up to the light.

"Let me see it," the girl said, "give it here." I backed up to the wall.

"Go on, do what you're told, give it to her," said the mother.

"It's mine," I protested, and held it behind my back, ready to run.

Before I could move, the mother pulled the card from my hands and passed it to her daughter. I wanted it back! I scurried around the table to where the girl stood holding my card up high in the air, smiling. "Give it to me, it's mine," I yelled and jumped up at her arm.

"La la la," she taunted.

And I jumped higher and yelled louder, "It's mine!"

A hand swooped onto my shoulder and spun me around. "Stop it, stop it!" the mother screamed, and her other hand came down again and again on my back, my face, my legs. I couldn't stand and I couldn't get away. "Do you hear me. Stop it!" I thought her eyes would pop out of her red face.

I looked round the room for the father, for someone, anyone, to help. Whenever I saw him, he was hidden behind a newspaper. I don't believe I ever saw his face except this one time when he lowered the corner of the paper and looked over the top. And it seemed for that split second, he was going to say something – but he didn't. I silently pleaded to him, but, pipe clenched in teeth, he turned back to his reading.

She let go so fast, I fell to the floor. Bent forward, hands placed on her knees, she panted, "Go outside, and stay out."

I stumbled along the passage to the garden.

It was a wet February day; my face stung and my body shook from fear and the freezing wet cold. I went into the smelly toilet and sat in that dark, spidery place until night came and I was allowed back inside and climbed the stairs to my room.

I don't know what happened to my card, but somebody knew where I was. I lay on my bed in the dark, shivering from the cold, and then I felt a warmth grow inside me. Somebody knew where I was.

★　★　★

My body shook from coughing and a sharp pain in my back kept me awake at night. Snot ran over my lips. I wiped it away with my jumper sleeves and wore my skin away. I had lost all my hankies and wasn't supposed to use my sleeve, so I crept into the girl's room to take one of hers. But God sees everything and I didn't want to go to Hell. I started to leave, then noticed her beautiful doll sleeping in a cradle. She wore a pretty dress. I walked over, ready to tear a piece off her skirt, but it was too pretty. I looked underneath at her petticoat. It was made of pink net, and I tore a piece off with my teeth. It was very scratchy and the net was too full of holes to be any good. The girl never told on me.

Nobody noticed my nose until I spat on my baby Jesus drawing to rub a crooked line away, and out came thick, green globs of slime.

"Come here, child," Sister Ann said. She wrapped her black shawl around my shoulders and rushed me out of class to my foster home. The mother was not at all pleased to see us.

"I'll fetch a doctor," Sister Ann said.

"Upstairs, you," said my foster mother. "Trouble from the first," she mumbled. I followed her to the bathroom. She scrubbed my face and rubbed the cloth around my neck. "Here, put these on," she said, and threw me a pair of the girl's pajamas.

They were big, but they were soft and had long sleeves. I held the bottoms up as she called me to the girl's bedroom. A bed with white enamel spindles at the head and foot was placed in front of the fireplace. There were thick blankets on the bed and a fresh fire burned in the grate. "Hop in," she said. It wasn't my bed and I lay still, arms at my side, so as not to mess it up.

I felt the sheets smooth against my chin, felt the blankets so thick they pressed me into the soft mattress. There was a pillow too, soft like the one I remembered from home. I felt dirty lying in this clean bed, a trespasser, like when Patsy jumped over the fence at the apple tree house.

The doctor arrived. He listened to my chest and sighed and said to put hot compresses on it and keep me warm. "Give her this, three times a day," he said handing the mother a bottle, "and put some Vaseline on that nose of hers. I'll be back tomorrow."

"You'd better contact her mother," he said as he left.

He had a kind face. I wanted him to take me with him. I wanted him to look at me. I stared at him. My eyes followed his every move, trying to make contact. But, like all grown-ups, he didn't see me, and I was too afraid to speak. He came the next day and the next, and all he did was sigh.

Mummy finally arrived, she brought some hankies for me, and a doll. "Sorry to worry you Mrs. Kelleher," I heard the foster mother say as they walked up the stairs. "She's much better today, though." She tapped the bedpost with her long claw-hands.

"I'll leave you alone then. Bring up a cuppa in a minute."

"Hello, Joanie, how are you feeling?" Mummy came alongside the bed and put the palm of her hand on my forehead. It felt soft and warm.

"What a nice room you have." I couldn't tell her it wasn't mine. I couldn't say anything except, "Hello, Mummy."

"I've managed to find you a doll. It's your birthday present," she said, placing it by my side. I knew it was a boy because it wasn't pretty. His hair was painted on, and he had no clothes, not even a blanket.

"Thank you, Mummy." She smiled and patted my hand.

Mummy stayed with me the whole day and put hot compresses on my chest. I felt the warmth going right into my body. The sharp pains eased, and I could breathe. She sat quietly by my borrowed bed, saying very little beyond "Feeling better?" and I dozed off and on, and lay as still as possible, self-conscious, uncomfortable, embarrassed for being a nuisance.

The room became dark, and it was time for her to go, before curfew. She kissed my forehead and said, "Be a good girl, now." I couldn't smell roses.

★ ★ ★

I didn't care much for the doll. His fingers were sharp, his body stiff. He didn't feel friendly at all. What's the good of a doll if it can't be dressed or cuddled? I looked across the room at the girl's doll lying in a pink doll bed and wished that pretty doll, with the curly hair and fluffy dress, was mine.

The fire went out, the compresses went cold and felt wet and heavy. The foster mother didn't make any more.

★ ★ ★

As soon as I came in from school, I went straight to the kitchen to eat my tea. I'd eat quickly, before somebody came into the room. Sometimes the mother was there, peeling vegetables or washing dishes. I kept my eyes lowered and ate as fast as I could, picking up every crumb.

"Waste not, want not," that's what the mother said.

Once in my room, I listened to the silence. I was told to keep my door shut but I left it ajar, just a bit, so I could see the light from downstairs glowing faintly through the banisters and reflect off the wall outside my room. The narrow bars of light kept the cold dark from crushing me.

The smell of food cooking floated in through the cracked door, even boiled cabbage smelled wonderful. I'd imagine the family sitting by the fire, cozy and warm, while the father read his paper and smoked his pipe. And I'd sit on my bed, arms wrapped around my knees, or lay under the blanket, creating multiple variations of my fairy-story family: Mummy and me, sometimes Patsy.

★ ★ ★

At school, during playtime, I moped around, lost and lonely, longing for a friend. Most of the girls at school were already friends, and us evacuees just stood around, uninvited strangers. Outsiders. Invisible. We didn't even see each other.

The boy did speak to me once when I came in from school.

"Hey, you." the boy said. "Do you know Hitler's going to kill all children who don't have blue eyes? It says so right here, in the paper. Your eyes are green. Irish eyes." He said it like Irish eyes were the very worst eyes to have.

Patsy's eyes were big and green and beautiful, like Mrs. Cooper's old cat, but I'd never seen my eyes and had no idea what "Irish" meant. My mother had blue eyes and I wondered if I could talk to Hitler (whoever he was) and tell him, if that would count.

I went to my room and began to worry about Hitler. I had heard people call him a "monster," maybe that's why he wanted to kill children, like the baby Jesus and King Harold, or was it King Herod? And he could be any-where. My skin prickled, my stomach tightened. I looked around my room. The boxes stared back, silent, dark. I closed my eyes and tried to think of my mother, remember a fairy story, but all I could think of was a monster named Hitler who was coming to kill me.

I curled up on my side and forced myself to think about sunshine and how it felt when it warmed my skin, about horses and their soft noses and big brown eyes, fat round robins, my friend Ted. I kept my mind busy with thoughts and questions, and discovered I liked to think, especially about things for which I had no answers, which was practically everything: how does the sky change colour...what holds the rain in the clouds before it comes down...where does the sun go during the night...where do stars go during the day. It was very satisfying to leave my mind open, with a thought sent out into the night, waiting for a response from someone unknown with answers that I could accept or ignore, or better yet explore, which led to another thought and another question.

★ ★ ★

Soldiers break into my room. They wear armor and have long spears, like the soldier in Mrs. Croft's picture. They know I'm there, but I can fly. I fly up to the ceiling and lay on my back arms outstretched, not breathing; they start to leave. The last one turns around, he sees me, and they come back on horses, poking their spears up at me, trying to kill me. I push myself against the ceiling with all my might, pushing it higher and higher and they get smaller and smaller. I wake up, shaking. But they didn't get me.

They will never get me.

CHAPTER 11

THE DISAPPEARING HOUSE

"The really exciting part," said Eeyore in his most melancholy voice, "is that when I left it this morning it was there, and when I came back it wasn't. Not at all, very natural, and it was only Eeyore's house. But still I wondered." A.A. Milne

While I was allowed to walk to school alone, every Sunday morning the same two mothball nuns arrived at the house to take me to Church. Going to Church was another thing that made me different from this family.

My foster mother told me to stand by the door and wait for the knock, as if she did not want the nuns to enter her house. No breakfast in case they came early. I didn't like going to Church. I couldn't understand the priest at all, so it wasn't interesting. It was cold in there too, and kneeling hurt my knees and my stomach growled and embarrassed me to end. The nuns knelt on either side, blocking my view of other people and poking me with their sharp, pointy fingers when I tried to look around them, hissing, "Kneel up straight!" And when that didn't work, I'd get a whack from a prayer book on my bottom.

One cool spring Sunday, right in the middle of Mass, while we were kneeling down for the important part, where the priest mumbles away in Latin and we're supposed to answer, and the altar boy swings the incense burner (that was the part I liked best, the "clink-clink" sound and the sweet smell of the smoke), the church filled with deafening noise, as if bombs were exploding inside. The nuns grabbed my head and tried to push me under the pew, but I wriggled free. I wanted to see what was happening.

In open-mouthed wonder, I saw the coloured glass windows shatter inwards. Glass flew through the air, fast and slow at the same time. Tiny shards of red and blue glass flew in silence, looking like a broken rainbow as it fell to the floor. Then it was over, just as quickly as it had begun.

There was no siren sound, no all-clear.

I felt nothing, except surprise, and wondered if everyone that was bombed felt that way, like a spectator. Perhaps the waiting was far worse than the actual happening.

People yelling broke the silence. Caught up in the excitement, I stood up, ready to run, but the nuns held me back.

"Sit here, don't move," they said and pointed to the pew. I sat and waited in the empty church, which had been filled just a moment ago. How quiet it was, after all that noise, where has everyone gone? Why must I stay here? It seemed like a very long time before the nuns came back, and by that time, I felt numb all over, as if I were sleeping.

We left the church and walked even quicker than usual back to the house where I had been living.

The wind brought a strange smell with it, a moldy, wet smell. My legs were shaky, my whole self tingled. The street was very quiet, and the closer we got to the house, the stranger the house looked. Something was wrong. I stared and tried to figure out what it was. The walls were there, and the bird's cage swung in the window frame, but the walls were broken, and I didn't see the bird – just the empty cage. Wisps of smoke trailed up in the air and moved in the breeze. Piles of broken bricks littered the place that had been a garden just a short while ago. So full of questions, my mind could not form one complete thought. My mouth was open, but no sounds came. I felt sick from the smell of wet smoke.

The nuns looked quickly at each other and I looked up at them. But we kept on walking, not saying a word, as if I had not lived there, as if nobody had lived there, as if the house had not been there at all. How strange it was, how empty it felt. I kept my eyes on the broken house as we walked quickly by, craning my neck – looking for something to move, someone to appear. I wondered if the family was in their air-raid shelter. I could not ask. I could not utter a word.

We walked on in hurried silence, the nuns' rosary beads the only sound, jingling in rhythm with their swishing habits, and arrived at the big "holding house." They spoke in whispers with a grown-up, then left. Hugging my gas mask, I stood in the middle of a room as big as a whole house and felt my body start to shake.

There were lots of children in that room, evacuees like me, waiting for someone to take them in. They were sitting everywhere: on the wide staircase, on chairs, on carpets in front of a fire blazing in an enormous grate. We exchanged glances, but nobody spoke. Two big girls stood by the fireplace, talking behind raised hands, looking over at me with suspicious, unfriendly eyes.

"Here, dear, some Oxo," said one of the ladies, handing me a cup. She smiled at me.

I held the hot cup with both hands and felt the rich drink slide down my throat, warming by body and melting the cold in my bones. It was the most delicious thing I had tasted, ever. I asked for "more please," and watched her worried look before telling me there was no more.

I stood on the same spot all day, clutching my gas mask, staring into the fire, my mind filled with pictures of the broken house, until a billeting officer came towards me. A brown- shoed lady.

"We have a new home for you," she said. I stared at the whiskers sticking out of a huge brown mole on her chin. "Come," she said, putting her hands on my shoulders.

But I didn't want to go to another home. I wanted to stay here, with the smiling lady and the hot Oxo and the blazing fire, and stared down at the carpet, feet planted, refusing to budge.

"Come on, dear, be a good girl," she said, and taking my hand, pulled me out of the warm room into a waiting car.

* * *

This house was small, though bigger than a cottage. Yellow dandelions and long grass covered the front garden and the broken, wooden fence leaned in different directions than the creaky gate. The billeting lady banged on the brown chipped-paint front door with her fist. The door squeaked open and we walked into the dark house.

Three people stood in the kitchen, the mother, father, and a grown-up daughter, who stood with her head to one side, almost touching her shoulder, a string of drool hanging from her open mouth. I stared at her mouth, frightened, fascinated.

There was another evacuee, the billeting officer told me, a twelve-year-old boy, about six years older than me.

"Isn't that nice," she said.

The billeting lady told my new foster mother how to get new ration books, the government allowance, and "Yes, her mother will send you extra."

"Not much in here, I'm afraid," she said, handing over a bag of clothes. "Not much going spare."

They talked about me as if I wasn't there. I raged inside – a silent fury that made me shake. *I don't want to live with any more strangers. I don't want to be bombed and burned.*

I want to go home.

I want my mother.

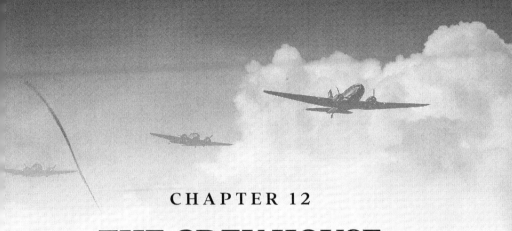

CHAPTER 12

THE GREY HOUSE

"Well," said Pooh, "we keep looking for Home and not finding it, so I thought that if we looked for this Pit, we'd be sure not to find it, which would be a Good Thing, because then we might find something that we weren't looking for, which might be just what we were looking for, really." A.A. Milne

I didn't hear their names. My ears were still ringing from the shattering glass. Besides, I didn't care who these strangers were. They didn't want me either, and I was going to run away soon. Other girls did, I heard about them at school. They didn't come back either.

"'Ello," said the mother. Her apron was dirty, the pocket hung half-off, her lips were cracked like the shell of a boiled egg. I turned away and looked at the father. He wore suspenders and a string around his waist. His crinkled face was whiskery. His head was shiny in the center where hair should be. He nodded his head at me, but I ignored him too.

All three looked tired, as if standing was an effort. The father, tall and skinny, leaned against the table, making a cigarette. The mother folded her arms across her sagging chest like the nuns did when they were angry, pressed her lips together and stared at me. The daughter's mouth was slack, open, and her beady brown eyes constantly moved, making up for the emptiness of the rest of her. She looked like a witch, and I took a step back and lowered my eyes.

I had only just met the billeting lady, but as the door closed behind her, I felt I'd lost my only friend.

I held my gas mask tight to my chest. I didn't want to cry, didn't want a "what for." I pretended I was invisible.

"I'll show yer the 'ouse," said the foster mother, hands now on hips. I followed her along the corridor. She opened the door to the dark living room. Dust covered the wooden furniture like cloth and sparkled in thin streams of sunlight as it floated around the room and got pushed around by the opening door. "Not allowed in 'ere. For special occasions only." We walked through the kitchen into the scullery, which contained the single sink in the house, big and square.

"This is where yer wash," she said. "There'll be no 'ot water – not boiling kettles for washing faces."

The lavatory was opposite, with one tiny window up high in the wall. I took a peek at the garden out back. There were no flowers, no shelter either, just dug up earth, black and lumpy and bare. A tiny square of lawn on the side of the house edged with violet flowers was the only colour to be seen. Everything about the house and garden looked old and dull, as if it was wrapped in a cloud of grey. Even the people looked faded, especially the grown-up daughter, who seemed like her mother's shadow.

It smelled old too, musty and moldy, like rotten cabbage and blocked-up drains. I shuddered from the smells, from the feelings that crept over me from this dead house, these tired strangers. *I don't want to be here*, my whole being screamed.

The mother called the boy evacuee in from the garden. "Take 'er upstairs," she told him.

He smiled at me. His eyes were blue like my mother's, and he was tall and thin like Patsy. He smiled – I stared. He said "Hello," and offered to carry my gas mask up to the bedroom we would share. I clutched it to me. You weren't supposed to go anywhere without it.

There were three bedrooms upstairs. The room we were to share was at the end of the dark corridor. There were no lights that I could see, not a bulb anywhere. I looked at the window criss-crossed in tape, the wooden chair and the narrow bed alongside the wall. I smelled the damp, sour room and stared at the broken linoleum covering the floor, the rumpled blanket on the bed, the striped pillow. I clutched my gas mask tighter.

The bomb had dropped only that morning. It seemed such a long time ago. I mustn't think about that. Nobody had mentioned it. Perhaps nobody knew but me. I wouldn't tell. Maybe they did and were angry because I left the house to go to church. And maybe it *was* my fault the bomb dropped. I didn't like any of them, not even the father. What did Sister Theresa say about "bad thoughts being the same as bad deeds?" Perhaps I had committed a mortal sin and would be sent to Hell. Maybe my candle had been turned upside down and I had been excommunicated. Whatever that meant.

★　★　★

The nuns never came to this house, so I didn't go to Church. I didn't mind. I could never talk to God in Church anyway. The priest did all the talking. God listened to me when I was by myself, though I prayed to Jesus, except when the sirens screamed, then it was God. Sometimes, when I sat or stood really still, I could feel Him, or an angel, someone standing behind me, just behind my left shoulder. Someone tall and light and soft and gentle. I wished I could feel my angel now.

Standing in that dark room, I decided being invisible wasn't enough anymore. From now on, I would hide as well, until I could run away, home.

★　★　★

"Miss Fussy," the mother said when I didn't eat my tea. I wasn't hungry and felt sick just looking at it.

She had dropped the lumpy porridge into my bowl, and there it sat, a lumpy grey mass until the steam was replaced by a film of slime. Globs splattered on the table, which she scooped up and put back in the pot.

After tea, I crept upstairs and stood, hands tight behind my back, staring at the boy lying in bed. I wasn't sure about sharing my bed. True, I had shared with Patsy, but she was my sister. This was a stranger – and a boy.

He smiled. "Come on then," he said, patting the crumpled cover.

I stood behind the thin dusty curtain, pulled a huge nightie over my clothes and climbed slowly on the bed. On the outside. No sooner was I in it, than he pulled down the blanket, and his pajamas, saying "I'll show you mine, if you'll show me yours," or something like that.

I looked down in spite of myself and saw what I thought were some interesting knobbly bits in the place where I knew I was flat. While curious, I knew this was not a good thing, said a firm "No!" crawled under the cover to the foot of the bed and poked my head out the end. He gave me the pillow and never asked again.

And this is how we positioned ourselves the remainder of our time, sharing that bed.

Sleep would not come. I heard the shattered glass, smelled the smoke, saw the broken house where I should have been. I lay on my back, arms stiff at my side, eyes squeezed shut, but I still heard the bombs explode in my head and jumped up ready to run. Every time I jumped, the boy spoke to me, softly, gently. I didn't hear the words, but his voice brought me back to the present and to bed.

After nights of lying on guard half-awake in our shared bed, I began to feel safe and finally slept. He was big and, like Patsy, could keep the things that live in the dark from finding me. I knew he would wake me up if there were bombs.

Every night he talked to me. "I've always wanted a little sister," he told me. He was an only child. He said he was pleased to have someone around to talk to, that he missed his parents. I faked sleep and seldom responded beyond "um," but I listened. I lay awake for as long as I could so I could listen to him breathe the soft breath of sleep.

I soon became used to sharing my bed, it felt like I had Ted or Patsy near me, and I got to sleep on the outside too. Some mornings I would awaken, rolled up in our thin blanket, stolen during the night. The boy never complained. Just like Patsy, I thought, when I climbed over her to sleep on the outside edge of our bed in the cupboard under the stairs.

★   ★   ★

To my relief, the grown-ups ignored me. At the other foster home, I had to stay in my room, "out of sight," but I wasn't told what to do in this house. Only the boy spoke to me, but just to be sure, I tiptoed around, lurked in dark corners, hid outside in the garden shed. The shed was made from wooden boards, with narrow spaces in between. Filled with old buckets and garden forks and spades and sacks of rubbish, it was the best hiding place. No one went there, came looking for me, or even called my name. Perhaps they hadn't noticed me at all or didn't care that I was living in their house.

I pretended the shed was my cottage, and I wanted it to smell like home, so I picked up petals from the purple flowers that had fallen to the earth and put them in an old jam jar with some rainwater I got from a large wooden barrel. I was going to make a scent of roses. I could hardly wait to take off the top, but when I did, the petals were brown and slimy and the water smelled dead.

Spiders lived with me, but they stayed in their webs up high in the corners. Beetles scurried around the earthen floor, black beetles, brown beetles, all of them shiny. I sat on the ground, a turned-up flowerpot my table and pretended they had come to visit, "Would you like some tea, Mr. Beetle?" I picked one up, a small black one, maybe a baby I thought. I held him loosely in my hand and watched his beady eyes and long eyebrows move up and down and around. His scratchy feet tickled my hand and I put him down, gently, and watched him scurry away. If Mr. Croft were here, I'd ask him if beetles were important, like worms and bees. Though it didn't really matter, I'd add them to my list of friends anyway. Spiders I was not so sure about. I knew they had saved Jesus, but they were always watching me and seldom moved, just watched, with dark, knowing eyes.

Two chickens were cooped up behind a wire fence, back of the kitchen wall, a white hen and red rooster. Chickens! "How are you today, Mrs. Hen?" I asked. They were always busy scratching the earth heads in the air as if praying for a juicy worm, then they'd peck, peck, peck at the ground and scratch some more. Neither one of them looked at me, not like horses, but I still talked to them and watched their bright eyes dance and blink and was sometimes rewarded with a clicking sound I pretended meant "Hello."

★　★　★

Every day it got a little colder, a little darker in the shed. The beetles began to hide. Shadows chased each other around the walls, wind whistled through the boards, and my place of refuge became less inviting. Since nobody seemed to care where I was, perhaps they would not care if I were in the house. So I found other hiding places inside where I would stay, waiting for the evening meal or bedtime.

The lavatory became another favourite hiding place of mine. Torn sheets of newspaper, tied with a string hung on the wall, waiting for use. I looked at the small print, squinted, tried to make out words. A tiny window was the only light, but that's how I learned to read. It took a long time, but one day I could read like a grown-up without stopping between the words.

★   ★   ★

The ladies at the "holding house" had given me a bag of used underwear, a jumper and a coat. The coat was much too big and heavy around my neck. My foster mother rolled up the sleeves, saying, "There, that's better." But it wasn't. My arms were in splints. As soon as I was out of sight, I shook the sleeves down. Walking up and down the garden swinging my arms, waving the loose ends of the sleeves in front and behind me, I pretended they were the wings of a bird and I could fly. I'd fly over the housetops to where the horses waited for me in the field with the big green trees.

I still had my own shoes. The backs were split, and nails poked through, but I curled my toes under and kept them from poking me, until the sole came loose. For a while, I walked with the flapping sole. Raising my foot high, plunking it down on the ground all at once, like a soldier, marching. Plunking and flapping was fun, like jumping in puddles – much better than walking properly. The fun ended when the soles fell off. The father tried to fix them. He put my shoes on an iron frame and tried to hammer in tiny nails. "No wear left," he said.

To the Charity Shop we went. The shop was set up in a church hall. Racks of clothes hung on crooked hangers, waiting for a new owner to exchange clothes or ration coupons for them. Ladies stood in the aisle, taking their clothes off and putting others on. They stood there in their underwear, corsets and vests and big knickers, and didn't hide. I walked under the racks, the dresses brushed my face and were soft and smelled clean.

"Now look wha' yer gorn an' done," my foster mother said. I looked at the floor and saw dresses I'd obviously knocked down. "Come 'ere, try on these Wellies." I didn't get a "what for."

There were no shoes in my size, it would be Wellington boots, green and smelly. I flopped around in boots too big and gripped with my toes so they wouldn't fall off, and with every step they slapped my leg as if they were chasing me.

The Charity Shop day was special, the mother took me on a bus, one without doors, the opening for getting on and off at the back. I looked out the opening and saw people whiz by in a blur of colour and felt a fast, fresh wind on my face. Two ladies sat opposite making "tutting" sounds, "Poor little mite," and, "She looks so pale." One of them offered me a piece of chocolate. I shook my head "no." My body told me I should not eat it.

"Don't be rude, this 'ere is special, this is," said my foster mother, digging me with her elbow. After the first swallow my stomach turned to liquid and a hard lump pushed at my throat. I ran to the doorway just before the chocolate came back up. The two ladies made such a fuss. "Sorry missus," they said. My face was hot and cold at the same time, my head thumped, my eye hurt, my legs wobbled. I wanted to lay down. I braced myself for a "what for" which thankfully never came.

Headaches attacked me in the middle of the night, at school, after air raids. If there was any food in my stomach, up it would come. I always managed to hold in the sick until I was outside or in the lavatory. And every time my head split in two, I numbed myself to whatever was going on around me until I could sleep.

★ ★ ★

This third family had very short conversations, usually two words long – wake up, clean up, hurry up – with lots of grunts, and "aye's" and "nay's." So, it was a surprise when I heard the mother and father talking about their hen.

"She's just broody," snapped the mother.

"Nay, not this time, 'er is sick," said the father, "castor oil 'ill fix 'er up." He reached into the narrow kitchen cupboard and took out a bottle. "Get us a spoon then."

"Get it yerself, I ain't got time for messin' wi' 'ens."

"I'll do it, please, I can do it," I pleaded, and ran to the drawer and picked up a spoon.

Out in the garden we went to catch the hen. As soon as the fence was opened, off she sped, as far away from us as she could get. The old man wasn't very fast on his feet and the garden was lumpy, and as he slipped and tripped, I shooed her until, huffing away, he finally caught her. Old hen looked as frazzled as old man, but he smoothed her feathers speaking softly,

"There then, it's alright," and tucked her under one arm, forcing her beak open with the other, while I poured the oil down her scrawny throat.

"There's a good hen," I said, empty spoon in hand, glowing with importance.

She kicked up such a fuss, even when she was put down, flapping her wings and wiggling her tail, all the while making screeching noises, and the rooster got very angry. He flew at my face with his beak and claws going like mad to punish me for hurting his beloved hen. His claws scratched my face and he pecked my head hard, making it bleed, while his wings flapped furiously around my ears. He was strong and I couldn't get away until the old man grabbed him.

That evening, while I sat in the lavatory, I heard a sad croaking coming from a cardboard box full of rags and old sacks placed alongside the wall. I knew immediately what it was. I knew about people buried alive and dying from lack of air. I wanted to rescue him but knew I was not supposed to know. Could I have caused this unhappy end for a rooster who was only protecting his hen? It was a horrible thought and gave me nightmares for ages, where once again the scrawny rooster was scratching my face and pecking my head for killing him. I went to bed and cried for the rooster, poor old, skinny old chicken.

The hen disappeared, too. They weren't buried in the garden, but nobody ate them either. I would have remembered eating meat.

Weeks later, the father walked into the kitchen carrying a shopping bag. He never went shopping, and I watched while he emptied the bag onto the kitchen table. Out popped chicks, round balls of yellow fluff, chirping loudly for their mother. So much noise coming from such tiny little beaks. They ran around on the old oilcloth, making tiny circles, bumping into each other in their haste. I reached out to touch one, but the father said not to as I might make them upset, so I just watched and laughed at these tiny little beings. There were twelve. "Why twelve?" I asked.

"Well," the father said, rolling a cigarette paper between his fingers, "yer need a dozen if yer want six." That made absolutely no sense, none at all, until he added that you have to allow for the ones that will die. With that depressing thought, he allowed me to pick them up, one at a time, and deposit them behind the chicken wire on the bald part of the garden, alongside the neighbors' fence. I could feel their little hearts beating against my hands, their tiny feet scratching my skin. I put each one down, with a kiss on its head, and watched them start scratching the earth.

My job was to make sure they had water in the old, cracked dish. Every day after school, I rushed home to take care of the chickens. Every day, there was one or two lying down, unmoving.

The father was wrong. He didn't get six, not even one. He should have bought more.

CHAPTER 13

THE MAKESHIFT SCHOOL

"Do you know what A means, little Piglet?"
"No, Eeyore, I don't."
"It means Learning, it means Education, it means all the things that you and Pooh haven't got. That's what A means." A.A. Milne

"**S**chool today," the mother told me. "'E'll take yer," she said, nodding her head in the boy's direction.

The boy reached out his hand to me, but I didn't take it. He walked slowly so I didn't have to trot to keep up and left me outside huge black iron gates and told me to wait there for him after school. But this wasn't my school. There was not a field or tree in sight. Not a hawthorn bush. Not the song of a bird. And no horses. I tried to tell him, but he kept on walking, his back to me, waving his hand "goodbye."

I stared at the ugly, low red-brick building. The playground was black asphalt, edged in a spiked black iron fence. Air-raid shelters filled up most of the space. They looked like concrete boxes, dark and damp, with zigzag entrances and no windows.

I didn't like this place one bit. It didn't look like a school at all. They've made a mistake. I shouldn't be here. I looked around to see where I could hide until the boy came back. I could hide in the shelters, but I don't like the dark and the things that lived in the dark. There were shops around a square and grown-ups who would tattle if they saw me. And if I got caught, they'd call me a truant and take me to the police station, and I would be in very serious trouble. That's what had happened to Jennifer. A police lady had brought her back to school and Sister Theresa gave her three whacks on her hands. She didn't play truant again. Jennifer was always in trouble for no reason at all that I could see. She was very fat, with teeth that poked out like a rabbit, but that's no reason to punish someone. Maybe the nuns thought she was pulling funny faces at them. Funny faces and raspberries always made them angry.

Who said I must go to this school? Why did I have to be here? I could just walk away, and once I decided that, my arms popped out with goose bumps and I suddenly felt brave. I started to walk out the gates, taking tiny steps, when cries of "fight, fight!" surrounded me and a pack of boys came running towards the open double doors of the building. I got caught in the rush as they pushed me along into a huge dark room already overflowing with children.

Two boys punched and kicked each other, and other boys yelled and pushed to get a closer look. A big girl yelled, "Teacher's coming!" And there she was, a fat, puffing, red-faced, suited lady. She grabbed an ear of each of the fighting boys and dragged them, on their tiptoes, out the back door yelling, "You lot, sit down!" Nobody did, not until other teachers entered the room. The boys and big girls disappeared behind wooden screens, which sectioned off the huge room for different age groups and boys from girls.

I hid in the shadows, biting my nails, stomach churning. I slid along the wall, back towards the door, feeling my way with my hands – I still had time to get out of the room, they wouldn't miss me if I... In bustled another teacher with heavy, laced-up shoes and scraggly grey hair, stick in hand. Not a thin cane, but a thick, dark stick. Everyone scrambled to desks – silence.

"You there, what's your name?" I looked around. "Yes, you!" My whispery voice stuttered my name. Tapping her stick on a desk in front of her, "Here," she said. A prisoner again, I sat at a desk in front of the class with the other under-seven-year-olds (the babies). Two to a desk and "mustn't fidget." I tried to sit still – hands folded, legs dangling, staring at the smudgy blackboard, trying to think up new ways to escape this dusty, crowded room full of nasty smells of unwashed bodies, wet wool and stinking feet.

★　★　★

People walked by outside the iron railings. Freedom was only a railing away. All I needed to do was walk out the gate and keep on walking all the way to London. The street signs were gone, but I could follow the train tracks, they would surely go to London. Dick Whittington and his cat, they had found London. *But what if I get lost? What if the sirens scream? What if Mummy is angry with me for running away?* A whistle blew. Back to the classroom I went. For the rest of the day, I sat and sulked, angry with the coward that lived inside me.

School over, I waited outside for the boy. "How's school?" he asked.

"It's the wrong school. My school is by the horses, the Salesian School."

"They said that's too far away now," he said. "You'll like it, you'll see. It won't take long to make new friends." But I'd never had a friend. I didn't know how to make friends. And I hated this new school. And who were "they" anyway? That's what I wanted to say, but I looked at the ground, scuffed my feet and dragged myself back to the grey house.

Sleep would not come. I waited, tried to keep still, keep my eyes shut, but all I could think of was this old, grey house, the makeshift school with the noisy children and grumpy teachers and how much I missed Ted. He always made me feel brave, and he was gone. Then I thought of the horses in the fields, they made me feel brave – happy too. I made a plan and fell asleep.

The boy left me at the iron gates and reminded me to wait there for him to take me home. I nodded but did not answer. It was the longest school day ever. I didn't hear a word the teacher said, all I could do was try to look attentive while I waited for the bell to sound and I could start my adventure.

As soon as we were dismissed, I ran around the corner and took the first street I came to. There was an old man walking his dog, and a lady on a bicycle, but nobody else. I could see the tops of trees to my left and walked quickly towards them, must not run, people would know I was running away. My hunt for the trees took me on a winding walk, each street getting narrower until it became a lane. And there, in front of me, was a green field fenced in by a dark green hedge, and behind the hedge – horses. I ran across the street, stood in front of the hedge and counted. There were three horses, nibling sweet grass, and on the hill, under a tree, stood a huge horse, the colour of chestnuts, looking right at me. She seemed to be calling me. I wanted to touch her beautiful face.

There was a break in the hedge big enough for me to squeeze though. Branches snagged my clothes, but I kept going until I entered the field. I started to walk slowly towards her, but she came cantering down the hill towards me, her mane and tail streaming behind her. The earth seemed to shake under my feet, and I stood, frozen in fear, as she slowed to a trot and stopped in front of me. She blew through her wide, wet nostrils, and I felt her graceful movement as she wrapped her magnificent head around my skinny shoulders and nibbled the back of my jumper with her lips. I felt the warmth of her body, sticky against my face, the sweet scent of her, her gentleness, her power. My heart opened and love flooded inside me, filling me, like my dreams of what it would be like when I finally met my family again.

"There you are." It was the boy. The horse released me, and the spell was broken. He promised not to tell on me, if I promised not to come back here, ever again. "It's dangerous," he said. That this field belonged to somebody important, and these were his very valuable horses, and I was trespassing. Trespassing, "thou shalt not trespass." I knew that was a sin, maybe even a mortal sin. With a heavy heart, I promised.

The joy and peace this special horse had given me comforted me, made me smile on the inside. And I could bring it back whenever I felt afraid or lonely. It was almost as if Ted had found me again.

★　★　★

We stood to attention in the playground. Rain dripped off the tip of my nose, and a tall, fat man with a pointed beard blew a whistle for "Silence!" and talked until water squelched in my Wellies and my legs hurt.

"Discipline," he said, "that's what will win this war. Discipline. Pay attention, work hard and do what you're told." And to emphasise his point, he slapped the side of his leg with his stick. I looked around at the others nearby. They were not smiling or joking, they paid attention to the bearded man. His name was Head Master.

★　★　★

We sat "up straight," and spoke only when asked a question, "speak up, stop mumbling." I kept thinking of the shattered church glass, the noise, the bombed house, and I would see the broken bricks, smell the wet smoke. A bang on my desk brought me back, and the girl sitting next to me jumped in the air and shrieked with me.

I longed for the teacher to make that scratchy sound with the chalk, then I could say "ooh" with the rest of the class.

"Stand up and read the first three words on the board," the scraggly teacher told me. I stood up and stared at the letters sloping down the board, white letters on a grey board. I knew my alphabet but didn't know how to make words from these lines. I stood there while girls sniggered at me. My face burned.

"Glasses, that's what you need, my girl," the teacher said. I was too ashamed to tell her I didn't know how to read.

I climbed on the school bus, the one that went to the clinic. I climbed in a big, black leather chair and the doctor pushed a huge, black metal mask in front of my face. I held my breath as he fiddled with round pieces of glass and knobs on the side of the mask and asked me to look at the letters and numbers on a chart. "Which is clearer? This or that?" Every time he switched the knobs or glass, he said the same thing, and by the time he said "that" I couldn't remember what "this" looked like. It felt like a test at school. My palms became sticky with sweat. I knew he was getting impatient and I started to answer quicker, which seemed to please him.

I was fitted with thick lenses in black wire frames with springy earpieces that were much too big for me. I walked with my head held back to keep them on and when I needed to look down at my desk, put my finger in the middle of my nose to keep them from sliding off. They were a right nuisance and most of the time they were covered in smudgy fingerprints. The boy taught me how to "haaa" on them and wipe the sticky marks off on my skirt.

★ ★ ★

We didn't say prayers in this school. We did repeat the times tables, but I was bored with them by now and played a game where I added the numbers in my head to get the answer. Sometimes the teacher draped an oilcloth map of the world over the blackboard. "See all the pink bits," the teacher said, pointing with her stick, "those are ours. How much is ours?" she always asked. And we yelled, "Two fifths, Miss." And she tapped her stick on her hand, and paced up and down in front of us, looking important and pleased with herself. I loved the map and the click-click sound as she pointed to oceans and lands. The map bent with her stick. I loved it as much as adding the times tables and knew that one day I would travel to all those pink and brown and green places with exciting names.

★ ★ ★

This school did have one thing, paper, and we shared books, two to a book – torn, with missing pages, but still they were books with stories and poems. The paper was thick and yellow, with ragged edges, and handed out with, "Do your best work. There's no more where this came from."

We used real pens sometimes, too. But they were scratchy and made holes in the paper and dripped black ink over fingers and paper and desks. The inkwells were in little holes at the top of each desk and girls took turns to fill them up from a big pot, which the teacher first mixed with black powder and water. I wanted to do that. I wanted to wipe off the blackboard too and bang the pads together and make clouds of dust, but everyone did, and hands were raised in the air at the end of each day with cries of "Please, Miss, Miss!" Only the biggest girls were chosen.

With this gift of paper, the teacher decided I must use my right hand. "You'll never be able to use scissors," she told me. "I'm not allowed to use scissors," I wanted to say. But she placed my left hand behind my back, pressed into the back of my chair, and every time it tried to take the pencil from my right, the cane came smashing down on my desk, but never my hand. I noticed the teacher's stick was shorter than the nuns' and didn't swish as much. I wondered if it hurt more or less. Though I didn't want to find out. I never did get caned in this school. It seemed only boys were punished and the Head Master did the punishing.

Break time, and I was pushed out onto the black asphalt yard, where I stood against the wall. Girls and boys ran around and made noise, whistles blew to stop fights. There were no jumping jacks. It was raining that day. Grown-ups called it "drizzle," but I called it "sprinkles," like when Mummy shook sugar over my mashed banana and little flakes of sugar sprinkled down. Puddles formed like small oceans in the holes in the black asphalt, and raindrops splashed up like in a dance. Rain made days different from each other. It made everything look different too, shiny and fresh and clean. Even rain's smell was clean, like it had washed the air on its way down. I loved rain.

"Go straight home, curfew's on. No dawdling!" ended each school day. I watched children laugh, talk to each other, hold hands, walk arm in arm, but I still hadn't made friends. There again, being invisible was my choice.

I wondered what it would be like to have a friend, hold hands, laugh with someone at the teacher with the big lump on her nose. You couldn't laugh about that on your own, a big lump on a nose was just sad unless you shared it. But the boy was always there, waiting for me. He made me feel brave. He was bigger than any of the bullies. And when I got my glasses, no one called me "four eyes."

★ ★ ★

"Joan Kelleher, come here," my teacher said, and I found myself loaded on the Clinic bus again. The bus that called at each school to collect the "dirty" children, the ones everyone whispered about, with lice and boils and scabies and sores and ringworm, and took them to The Clinic. I had warts on my left hand, growing over my knuckles and under my chewed nails, that's why I was going. That's how I learned to tell my right from left hand, too.

We arrived at an old red-brick building in town with large wooden doors and a long white corridor. Children sat in bathtubs – shoulders hunched, puddles on floors. Sores covered their bodies and nurses scrubbed them with brushes. Others stood at sinks, getting their hair washed. Strong, nasty smells made my nose itch and eyes water. Cries of pain made my legs stiff and walk slower.

A nurse came up to me. "Come along with me," she said. All her clothes were white, even her hat and shoes and stockings. We walked into a small room where a lady sat, her hands resting on a white enamel bowl with dark-blue trim. She was one of the brown-shoed ladies I noticed.

"Soak your hand in there," the nurse said.

The water was very hot, and the lady held my hand down.

"Give it to me," the nurse said, and held my hand tight as she cut at the warts with sharp, shiny scissors. I saw my blood, a scarlet stream flowing into the bowl, swirling around in the clear water. *What are they doing?* I pulled my hand away and ran to the door, yelling, "I'm going to tell my mother!" I rattled the door so hard the frosted glass window shook. But I couldn't turn the handle, it slipped around in my wet grip, and the nurse came and led me back to the table.

"Let's put a bandage on that hand," the nurse said, just like nothing had happened. "We can make it better another day." *Oh no you won't, you try and I'll bite you. I'm going home to my mother.* That's what I wanted to say, but I thought it and held that thought in my head by squeezing my eyes and scrunching up my forehead.

When the boy met me after school, I kept my hand hidden. I kept it hidden in the house, which wasn't difficult as nobody saw me. That night, when the boy's soft breathing told me he was asleep, I started to dress. My Wellington boot dropped to the floor. I stood still in the shadows.

"What are you doing? Are you alright?" the boy asked, as he leaned up on his elbow.

"I want my mother. I'm going home."

"Hmm," he said, swinging his legs over the edge of the bed. "Do you know her address?"

"She lives in London, and we have roses in the garden." I looked at the floor.

"What about train fare? Do you have money?" he asked.

"I'll walk. I can walk all the way there," I said. But my stomach tightened when I thought of the dark outside the window and all the things that live in the night.

"It's a long walk," he said, "almost thirty miles."

I slumped to the floor and cried. I knew I couldn't go home. Maybe I'd never go home. Maybe Mummy didn't know where I was. Maybe I'd never see her again. He put his arm around my shoulders until my tears dried up.

★　★　★

This day at school, we had a real air raid, not just a false one or a drill. At the first sound of the siren, before it got really loud, the teacher banged her desk and blew her whistle, telling us to leave "in an orderly fashion," and go to the shelters. "Walk quickly, don't dawdle and don't run" and "don't forget your gas masks." We grabbed our gas masks off their hooks on the wall and ran, couldn't help it – once somebody started, you became part of the pack.

Grown-ups off the streets joined us in these shelters and we stood to-gether in that dark, crowded, unpleasant space until the all-clear sounded. Nobody uttered a word. It wasn't fun like the Salesian School shelter. We didn't repeat the times tables, and these shelters smelled like the spidery lavatory in the garden and made me feel sick.

I felt a pinch on my arm, a flick on my cold ear, an Indian burn on my wrist, but even though I looked around, I couldn't see who did it. All the girls were squirming, and all the boys were giggling. But you could never tell who it was, we were bunched together too tightly, and you couldn't yell, or the teacher would punish you and everyone would call you a "tattle tale."

On the way back into the classroom, a group of big boys sang a song:

"My teacher's got a bunion
A face like a pickled onion
A nose like a squashed tomato
And legs like matchsticks."

They sang it softly and laughed loudly and slapped each other's backs. It was a great song, and I wanted to remember it, so I hummed in my head during class and all the way back to the grey house.

★ ★ ★

War noise terrified me more than the bullies, the teachers, the nuns, my foster parents. I could feel my body tremble from the sound, as if I was part of what was happening and it was part of me.

The first time at my new house when the air-raid siren started, the boy whispered something I had never heard before, "Don't be afraid."

I didn't know I had a choice.

The sky never changed, though I expected it to. Some nights, stars filled the skies, bright lights sparkling against a soft sky, or there were more clouds, a fuller moon, but the sky always stayed the same no matter what the planes did.

I wondered if the sky would break one day from the fire and noise and fall down and bury us alive, or if the guns would kill the stars and leave a black hole. I told the boy I worried about the sky, the stars.

He told me not to worry. "First of all, the stars are millions of miles away, and anyway, the sky can't break," he said. "It has no ending."

CHAPTER 14

THE NOTHING TIME

Don't underestimate the value of Doing Nothing, of just going along, listening to all the things you can't hear, and not bothering.
A.A. Milne

Sometimes the father turned on the radio for the evening news. The mother and father leaned forward in their chairs, and the radio waves crackled and mixed with waves of concentration that I could feel. Nobody spoke. It was a reverent silence, like in Church.

The news people talked about ships exploding, soldiers in battles, invasions, bombs and how many people had died that day. They sounded important with their strong, teacher voices, "This is the BBC Home Service," like storytellers, but they never asked us how things were, so I wondered if they really knew what was going on. Even so, when they told us how many people had died that day, I felt a chill on the back of my neck, like goosebumps were pushing my hair out, and I'd say a silent prayer for my mother and Patsy to be safe.

Without the radio, the silence was loud. Every cough, the squeak of a chair, made me jump. The only soothing sound was the steady clickety-click of the mother's knitting needles as she knitted scarves that were never finished. I was sitting on a stool, one with three legs and placed in the kitchen corner behind the fireplace. The fire was small, poked a lot by the mother to keep it going.

"'Ere" she said, "I'll be catching me death soon, go fetch us some coal," and cocked her head towards the boy. I followed him out into the hall and begged him to let me come with him. "I can carry the bucket," I pleaded. He sighed and said, "Most of it I get off the railroad track. It's dark there." I said I didn't mind. "You promise to follow me and not run off?" I promised, and off we set.

Everything looked so different at night. There were no lights at all, not streetlights or lights from houses. It was dark and exciting outside. We walked to the railroad tracks, the gravel loose under my feet, looking for lumps of coal dropped from passing trains. It was like a treasure hunt, and when I found a large knob, I ran to the boy to show him. By the time we got back, I was ready to sneak upstairs to bed. But the mother was there, waiting.

"Look at yer, yer filthy," the mother said. I looked at my hands, they were black and everywhere I'd touched was black. "Go on then, wash up, and don't forget yer ears." She didn't give me a "what for" or tell me I was more trouble than I was worth. But she did tell the boy I wasn't to go with him again.

The longer the sirens were silent, the louder the silence became. Night after night, the silence increased, creating a time of slow, wasting nothing-ness, as if the world stopped and life had come to a standstill and the only thing to do was to wait – ready for…?

I sat on the stool, stared at the floor and chewed my nails and worried I might never see my mother again, never go home, that I would die from a bomb, or Hitler would find me and kill me because my eyes were green, or worse yet, stay here forever and become old and grey and shrivel up to nothing like dead flowers in a vase.

It wasn't a pretty walk to school either, mostly old shops on narrow streets and houses all built in that dead, grey colour. And ladies carrying shopping baskets, with scarves on their heads, tutting and moaning as they queued for food. I missed the fields where the green grass moved with the wind, the trees that sounded like rain, my horse friends and their soft, warm, velvet noses. I missed the birds nesting in trees, singing their songs.

I tried to remember the songs from the pictures Patsy had taken me to see, sing them in my head and pretend I was a beautiful lady in a long sparkling dress, as I kicked a pebble along the road in front of me, in the faded chalk boxes left over from a hopscotch game.

An old lady was walking towards me. She wore a pretty scarf around her neck, and I looked at it swirl. She smiled at me. Her smile was such a surprise; it meant she saw me. I didn't have enough time to smile back. I turned my head and watched her walk down the street. Maybe she was a fairy godmother. Maybe that's why she smiled. I looked for her every day. Next time I'd smile back, try to get her attention, make sure she saw me, and maybe she would wave her magic wand and give me three wishes. Or maybe she would follow me to my foster home and knock on the door. I'd give her my bread, then she'd know I was kind and I'd pass the test. Any old lady could be magic, though there were not many around. The ladies I saw were like my foster mothers, always in a hurry just to wait in a queue at the shops. But I practiced my three wishes just in case. My mother was always my first wish, then the others would change depending on how hungry or cold I was at the time.

★　★　★

The nuns didn't come to this house, so I no longer went to Church. Maybe I wasn't excommunicated; maybe they thought I was dead. I said my prayers to God and whispered my secrets, my fears to Jesus, and didn't miss going to Mass and getting poked by the nuns' boney fingers one bit.

With no Church to mark the week, Saturday and Sunday were like each other, with nothing for me to do. I sat in the lavatory as often as I could to read the newspaper pieces. The words went nowhere, but I didn't mind, it was fun making up endings and finding and sounding out new words. The mother gave me knives to sharpen in the earth, and I cleaned the stinking shoes. The shoes were heavy, too, and I made a fist to put inside the father's. They were always damp and warm from his feet and smelled like the chicken coop. But nothing was as fun as cat's cradle or stories.

The lavatory was still my refuge. Sitting there, on one of the nothing days, I noticed metal clips, holding the pages of newspaper together. They were shiny, pretty, and I started to pull them out, and when I had lots, I decided to clip them together, like a daisy chain. It was hard work without fingernails to help me, but very satisfying. It was the first thing I'd ever made. I was very proud and couldn't wait to show it to the mother.

"Where d'yer get that from, then?" she asked, and I proudly told her.

She didn't believe me, said it came from one of her looking glasses, "a chain for 'olding something up," she said. And it was confiscated, with a "might come in 'andy."

The mother and daughter were busy, when I saw them at least, though what it was they were busy doing was not clear, except drinking tea and saving things and knitting scarves that were never finished, never worn. The father too – every evening he emptied his pockets, removed his treasure of cigarette subs picked up from the streets and gently pushed the precious tobacco into a little tin, which he kept on the mantelpiece. Nothing went to waste in this house: little strips of sticky paper between postage stamps were carefully pulled off and hoarded, the daughter held moth-eaten jumpers in both hands, while the mother pulled on a thread and unravelled the wool into balls, knotted where the holes had been. Pieces of string were handled the same way, waiting to tie rags and newspapers into untidy bundles. Sour milk was shaken to death by the daughter, who tried to turn it into cheese. (I wondered where it came from; I'd never seen fresh milk in this house.) Her head to one side, mouth open, with a thread of spit dangling, but never dropping, she shook with all her might. I never saw the cheese. But then, I always left the room before she finished.

"Never know when *that* will come in 'andy," appeared to be this family's motto.

★ ★ ★

Spring. Daffodils. In the neighbor's front yard. Daffodils that raised their yellow faces to the branches of a scrawny tree just sprouting leaves, tiny white daisies poked up from the grass. If I could find the field again, of course, not the horse one, I might see snowdrops and bluebells and crocuses and foxgloves.

Birds sang a prettier song and fluffed their feathers – grateful the cruel winter was over. I placed my palms on the dirty bedroom window, warm from the sun. I wanted to talk – I wanted to sing – I wanted to dance!

I hummed *Daisy, daisy, give me your answer do*, my foster mother tutted, raised her eyebrows and tightened her lips. It seemed singing wasn't encouraged, as if it was inappropriate somehow – neither was talking, unless it was for a reason: "Did yer wash be'ind yer ears?" or "Time for bed," or the often repeated "Don't yer know there's a war on?" which always seemed silly to me. If there wasn't a war on, then someone was playing a bad joke on us all.

Perhaps my foster family was afraid and couldn't say so. They were old and very poor, that's what they said, "ain't paying that much for coal, money don't grow on trees, yer know." Perhaps it was harder for grown-ups because they knew things about the war and what it was like before – though I could not remember it being any other way.

Come six o'clock I was sent to bed. "Up yer go now," the mother said, and as I climbed the stairs, I heard the radio click on: "This is the BBC Home Service six o'clock news." The boy was allowed to stay up later. That's when he went hunting for coal. I missed our one-sided conversations, and I wanted to listen to the radio; sometimes there was music. The winter months were not so bad, as it was dark outside by six. But now it was summer and light until nine. The sun shone through the window and the tape pattern criss-crossed the entire room like bars on a cage. I longed for the dark to come and block out the bars and bring the boy upstairs.

I lay there, waiting – for the boy to come upstairs, for sleep to take me away, for a siren to scream. I stared at the stained wallpaper looking for shapes, pictures within the small, faded colourless flowers and trailing vines. I used watermarks streaking down the paper from the damp, the dark parts where pictures once hung, moved my head around, hung off the bed upside down, anything to expand the field of potential patterns. I could make out angels and witches and maps and tried never to see the same picture more than once.

And all the while, the birds sang and twittered joyfully outside in the soft evening sunlight, making me feel more awake and restless. My body and mind filled with longing – to the point of exploding – to be out with the birds, flying free in the evening's pink and purple sky.

Tears of frustration burned my eyes. I felt like the girl in the fairy story, locked in the tower trying to spin gold out of straw.

I made up stories about my family and what it would be like when we were all together again. Grown-up stories, not fairy tales, and I saw them in my mind, like the pictures Patsy had taken me to. I had to imagine what Mummy and Patsy looked like. I couldn't see their faces anymore.

I pretended how it might happen: we meet on the street and they recognise me right away… Mummy finds me, "Where have you been, we have been looking for you everywhere," "we thought you died in the bombs," she'd say, and take me away to our beautiful house… I find out where they live and surprise them all by knocking on the door, and Mummy kisses me and cuddles me and we all laugh, and they tell me how sorry they are that I have been alone for so long. Roses fill the rooms. We sit by the fire and have boiled eggs with soft, golden yolks and finger-stick bread… They call me "Joanie."

Sometimes I didn't want to daydream and I didn't want to play the wallpaper game, then a slow anger came over me, tightening my stomach, making my head buzz, seeping into my mind and taking over my thoughts, making me want to smash the window, tear down the curtains, kick in the door, run away through the fences and fields and never stop. But I knew I must never give in to Anger, the nuns had said it was a sin, except for God of course. We had to "turn the other cheek." I held my anger in, clenched my fists, my teeth. My head ached.

★   ★   ★

At mealtimes, the boy and I sat together in the kitchen, sometimes with the family. An old oilcloth covered the table, its pattern gone, worn thin from constant wiping and cracked in places so you could see the canvas backing. What we ate I can't remember, except porridge, bread, and sometimes powdered eggs, scrambled and dry. And one time we had the rind off a piece of cheese, I don't know where the cheese was, but the rind was there for the taking. The boy and I scraped the cheese from the cloth backing with our teeth. It was delicious. Of course, we must have eaten carrots and potatoes. I helped dig them up.

"Aye," said the father, when I asked to help. The boy gave me his fork and showed me what to do. Picking carrots wasn't particularly interesting; what you saw on top of the ground was what you got, one top, one carrot… now potatoes….

"Don't stab 'em," warned the father, "they be wasted if yer do."

Carefully, I put the large garden fork into the ground and balanced on top with both feet, felt it sink slowly into the black soil, turned the crumbly earth over and uncovered the prize —bunches of potatoes! I dug up a whole row of potatoes and counted each potato family. The big ones and baby ones, tied together with their stringy roots. The more I dug, the more excited I became, yelling to the world how many potatoes I had uncovered, each one in the telling, getting bigger than the last. It was like a treasure hunt. (I was always careful to cover the worms after we were through digging so the birds wouldn't kill them.)

The father sorted the potatoes, some for eating and some for replanting, put them in canvas sacks and stored them in the garden shed.

★　★　★

There was a strange smell coming from the kitchen when I got in from school, unpleasant, moldy.

"Come 'n get it," called the mother, and into the kitchen I went. Five chipped bowls waited, and the mother carefully spooned out a thick brown liquid in each. White curly things floated on top. Maggots! I pushed the maggot soup away and shuddered.

I remembered my first encounter with maggots at my other foster house. They were hiding in a potato. I was shaking with cold and hunger that day, and the hunger made me forget my fear and the promise of Hell for breaking the one commandment I did understand – all I cared about was finding something to eat. Creeping around the kitchen, I found a sack of potatoes in the larder. They wouldn't miss one. I picked it up and stuffed it into my mouth. Ignoring the dry dirt that clung to my lips I started chewing the hard, bitter tasting potato. Ready to take my next bite, I looked and saw fat, white, wiggly maggots. I got sick all over the larder floor and was given a "what for," then told to clean the mess up, which made me sick again. I had stolen that potato, so the "what for" wasn't a surprise – but I learned about maggots.

"It's bean soup, look," said the mother, eating a spoonful and making "um" sounds. The father raised an eyebrow as he slurped his bowl clean. I clenched my teeth tighter. I was not convinced. It just meant they were stupid enough to eat maggots, and I certainly would not, no matter how hungry I was. The boy finished his soup and smiled. At least he didn't try to persuade me.

"Waste not, want not," said the mother, and scraped my soup into her bowl.

Hunger made my stomach growl, in bed, at school, it growled for food. I tried not to think about it. It was better that way. If you thought about mashed bananas with sugar, or boiled eggs with their soft, golden yolks, or toast-teas, you would want to eat them, and if there were none, your stomach complained even more. Whenever I saw a hawthorn bush, I picked and ate the bread and cheese leaves; lots of children did. Patsy was always right.

Tar was fun to chew. I found that out when I saw children following a tar lorry, as if it held the Pied Piper himself. I watched them pick up the tar covering the potholes in the road and put it in their mouths. I picked up a glob too. It soon got hard, and the taste was strange, sort of peppery, but the chewing of it satisfying.

One lucky day, I saw a wad of chewing gum stuck to the pavement. I rushed to get it before anyone else. I wondered where it came from, only American's had gum and sweets, that's what the boy said. The gum was dry and tasteless, totally used up, but I enjoyed chewing it anyway, until I heard a loud "pop" and felt one of my teeth wiggle. I took out the gum and wiped my bloody hand on my jumper. I tried to sneak into the house.

"What's this? Open up, then," said the father. "Baby tooth." I closed my eyes, waiting for the slap. Instead, he found another use for the ball of string – and the kitchen doorknob – and told me I was a "brave little tyke."

"Gi' me that there jumper then. No use worrying the missus." I didn't see it again. Wasn't much wool left in it for saving.

★   ★   ★

Maggot soup was the only thing I got to share with Mummy when she came to this house. The foster family knew she was coming and had even dusted the living room, but I came in from school and there she was, my beautiful Mother. She had found me. She knew I wasn't dead.

My heart thumped. I felt a glimmer of hope. She might have come to fetch me. She was sitting in the "special occasion" living room with the foster mother, a cup of steaming tea in her hand.

"Hello, Joanie," she said, her eyes crinkled at the corners in a smile.

"Mummy," was all I was able to say. She looked so pretty, her curly hair clean and shiny. I breathed in her scent of roses, hungrily, greedily storing it in my head. There was no kiss.

"She likes school, Mrs. Kelli'er," sniffed the mother.

"Good girl, Joanie. Learn all you can."

I walked up close to where she was sitting, stood right in front of her, longing for her touch. "Are you being good?" she asked. I nodded and looked at the mother to see if she disagreed. But she just turned to go to the kitchen for more hot tea.

It was my opportunity, so I whispered to Mother, "She gave me maggot soup, but I didn't eat it."

"It were a nice bit o' bean soup," came the mother's voice from the doorway. "There was carrots in it too."

Mother smiled; she was convinced. (Grown-ups always stuck together.) But there was no "what for" for telling when my mother left. I was both surprised and relieved.

"Weather's nice," said the mother, as she poured more tea.

"Yes, especially for this time of year."

The grown-ups did all the talking, they always did, and when Mummy left this time, I didn't care.

CHAPTER 15

SKIES OF FIRE

You can't help respecting anybody who can spell TUESDAY, even if he doesn't spell it right; but spelling isn't everything. There are days when spelling Tuesday simply doesn't count.

A.A. Milne

Lights flashed through our thin bedroom curtain. Sirens screamed. I hid under the blanket, knees curled up tight, like a hedgehog poked by a stick. The boy rushed out of bed to the window and whispered, "Joan, come and watch." I was frozen in place. Noises filled my head so nothing else fit, just the noise. I wanted to run away but couldn't breathe. Light flooded the room, making it brighter than bright, penetrating my closed eyelids.

I kneeled on the floor, gripping the boy's leg, holding him tight so he won't go away.

"Look," he urged. I opened my eyes. This window was large, unlike the tiny eye at the other house, and seemed to project me into the sky, and I watched the heavy bombers flying overhead, and saw spurts of light from the "ack ack" guns, that's what he called them, firing from the ground. It was beautiful. It was terrifying. It was thrilling.

The sky filled with lights and shadows.

Drawn by the sights and sounds an arm's reach away, or so it seemed, we knelt on the floor, drew back the shabby curtain and stared at the sky before us, filled with airplanes and bursts of light and sounds of unending, echoing noise that shook the windows and bounced around the walls of our room. I placed my hands on the windowsill and felt the vibration from all the noise penetrate to every part of me.

I'd never seen so many planes before. Why? I asked him. He said we were just twenty-five miles west of London; there must be something special happening, though he didn't know what.

We whispered about what we saw and wondered out loud if any of the planes would crash around us. It was comforting talking with him about what was happening, especially as he knew so much about airplanes.

"See that one? The big one with four engines? That's a Stirling Bomber. You can tell by the short, wide wings. They use them as glider tugs too."

I did see it; it looked heavy and moved slowly. I listened to the names of the airplanes: Lancaster Bomber, Hawker Hurricane, Supermarine Spitfire, Bristol Blenheim, Gloster Gladiator. A first and a last name, like me. They sounded strong and brave.

"Those are ours," he told me. I wanted to know the names of "theirs."

"Messerschmitt, Junkers, Heinkels." Messers, Junkers, what silly names. None of "their" names sounded brave.

I wondered about the people in the planes, how they felt, if it was scary or exciting, and how brave they were up there all alone, taking care of us. I felt connected to the people in the planes somehow, almost like part of me was there, with them.

Watching with the boy was much less frightening than being alone, hiding in bed, squirming, waiting and listening in the dark, where my mind's eye took over my thoughts and changed every sight and sound into uncountable horrors.

"Good luck," he would say quietly when a formation of bombers and fighters flew overhead. I could see his eyes shining and wondered if they were tears.

★   ★   ★

There were air raids almost every night. I asked the father "why?" He mumbled obvious things like "it's dark." I didn't believe him. It would be easier to see the targets during daytime when it was light. At night, everyone had to obey the blackout rules, or the warden would come knocking on your door to remind you.

There were a few barrage balloons that came and went – they had the appearance of big, floppy, grey clouds, just floating, looking a bit sad and saggy, but they stayed there, until they were no more.

"Why are they there?" I asked the boy.

"Airplanes get tangled in the wires that hold them in place or explode if they hit them. They keep the Jerries away."

If that was so, I wondered why there weren't more.

On our way to school after a night of bombing, boys were running around the streets in frenzied delight looking for shrapnel, yelling at each other when they found pieces. Holding them high, bragging, pushing each other over in their eagerness. They scrambled over fences, into gardens, as they hunted for these chunks of broken metal and swapped them around. Hot pieces were the most valuable, it meant they were fresh – the larger the better. The boys tossed their new-found treasure from hand to hand, like in a game of "hot potato." Why do boys do such stupid things?

Then the nothing time would start again. Sometimes, I missed the air raids, the excitement, the terror, the quiet I felt inside when they were all over.

★   ★   ★

There were no air-raid shelters at this house; though some people had them, like my other foster family. There were no public shelters near us either, and no cellar in the house. We used the cupboard under the stairs.

When the bombing was heavy, someone thumped on our bedroom wall, yelling, "'Urry up." And all five of us would huddle in that tiny space, with its sloping ceiling, unpainted walls and sour smell. It was very dark, though a shaft of light flickered from a torch the father held, not turned on much to "save the battery."

Old winter coats hung from nails in the walls, smelling of mold and mothballs. Bundles of rags and newspapers tied with string were stacked haphazardly on the floor. But somehow, falling over each other in the dark, we fit. Balancing on the uneven surface of the bundles, we waited in stuffy silence until the all-clear siren moaned.

There was no air in the cupboard. I felt trapped and fought the screams that filled me. I tried hard not to touch anyone else or have anyone else touch me, and held my breath, tightening my stomach to make sure my lungs wouldn't move, feeling the blood filling my head, buzzing in my ears. Above all the noise of the airplane engines, the bombs dropping and the guns firing, I could still hear my heart beating and my silent prayer "Please God, please God" repeating over and over, vibrating through my body.

We stayed hidden until the all-clear sounded, keeping very still and silently listening, as if any noise we made would attract attention from the planes overhead and they would hone in on us and drop their bombs on the waiting target.

I could smell their fear, a sour smell like rotting leaves. The father breathed with his mouth open, and the daughter sounded as if she had just finished running a race, panting out hot air. How could I get out, past the others, and run away when a bomb dropped on us? I hated the cupboard under the stairs.

It should have been a relief to hear the all-clear sound, but I thought of the people who could be hurt. It might be me. I couldn't tell at first, as I was holding my breath for so long, I was numb. And it was such a mournful sound, like the bugle soldiers played at funerals on the radio – sad and lonely and empty.

After the all-clear, nobody spoke; we just knew what to do, and went back to bed, unless it was time to get up, then we would wash up for school.

The boy and I only washed the bits that showed, faces and hands, sometimes necks. He poured the ice-cold water into a chipped enamel bowl in the kitchen sink, and I'd stand on a chair and rub my rag over slivers of soap, there was never a whole bar. We didn't have to brush our teeth; there were no toothbrushes or toothpaste. I used my washrag to rub over mine. The mother and father soaked their teeth in a jam jar on the windowsill at night.

We washed occasionally, and only in the mornings. Most of us children had dirt rings around necks and wrists, with clean lines where the water had trickled down. With our scabby knees and yellow teeth, we could have been living in the same house.

★　★　★

A letter arrived, and the boy and I were called into the kitchen. The mother read it out loud. "I regret to inform you," she read, "during the air raid." I froze; my neck tingled. The boy's mother and father were dead, buried under the debris of their home. His father was a soldier, home for that day. I held my breath and watched the boy's face turn white. He did not utter a sound. I wanted to say something, but the words wouldn't form.

Our foster mother handed him the letter and told him to go and sit in the unused living room. It was "respectful to mourn the dead." So, there he sat, all alone for an entire afternoon, until it was time for tea. I sat on the staircase outside, listening. No sounds came through the door.

Nobody asked how he felt. He didn't cry. *What should I say to him?* I remembered how I felt when I lost my Ted. I knew he wanted to cry. He needed someone to cuddle him, to say kind words, but all I could do was support him with silence.

We ate our bread and drank our powdered milk tea. Nobody spoke of his parents. Neither did he.

That night we both lay awake in our shared bed. I waited for him to speak, like he always did, but this night we spent staring up at the ceiling, trying to see through the plaster and slate, through the dark night sky, looking for silver stars, searching for Heaven.

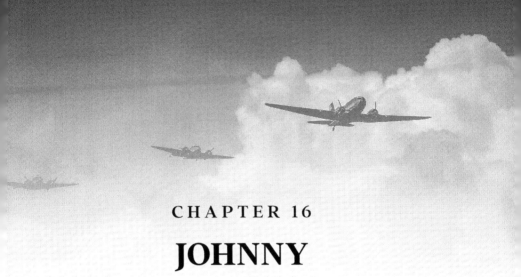

CHAPTER 16

JOHNNY

It's always useful to know where a friend-and-relation is, whether you want him or whether you don't. A.A. Milne

That year, my brother Johnny joined me in Chertsey. I was in class when a billeting lady brought a small, skinny boy into our room and introduced him to everyone, including me. I hadn't seen him since I was four, and he was a baby then.

"Take off your hat and sit down, John," said the teacher. He sat in the wastepaper basket and grinned from ear to ear. He took off his hat. His ears stuck out and his hair stuck up. He looked like an elf. The girls laughed. My face burned with embarrassment. The teacher banged her desk and the laughter stopped but the giggles began. Johnny pulled on his ears, poked out his tongue, wriggled his nose, made rude signs behind the teacher's back, and every time she turned around, there he sat, smiling like an angel.

The billeting officer soon picked him up again. There was no room at my foster parent's home, so he wouldn't be staying with me. We didn't get to say "hello."

A few months later, the mother announced Mummy was coming to take me to visit Johnny and meet his foster family. She must have sent a letter, but not to me. I wondered why she never wrote to me. Some girls received letters, they read them aloud and wrote a reply in class. The letter girl stood up, looked around at all of us with a smug smile, then read. All the letters started and ended the same, "My dear Mary, Jean, Maureen," and ended the same, "I miss you, love, Mum." I always listened and pretended I didn't care.

"'Ere, wash yer neck," the mother said, handing me my washcloth. I wiped the wet rag around my neck and up and down my dirt-stained arms.

Wild flowers grew in the empty lot down the street, and I went to pick some – totty grass, and daisies and buttercups and dandelions, the fluffy ones with "wishes." I admired the beautiful bouquet, especially the yellow in the buttercups and center of the daisies. It seemed they held part of a sunny day. I sat on the stairs, with the flowers in my sweaty hand, and as soon as my mother arrived, I handed them to her. My hands shook, waiting, hoping she would like them.

"How pretty," she said, and patted my shoulder. I felt the warmth of her touch go through my dress onto my skin.

We walked down the street together, side by side. This was the first time we had been alone together, except that time I was ill, and I kept looking up at her to make sure I wasn't dreaming. We stood in silence, a comfortable silence I didn't want to break. The bus came all too soon. It took us to the outskirts of town, just a few stops it seemed, but still a treat to ride on a bus, especially with my mother. I looked around to make sure people were noticing me and this beautiful lady, with her pearl earrings, dressed in pretty, clean clothes, with lipstick and curly hair and shiny shoes and smelling of roses.

Johnny had been placed on a farm owned by an older couple. Their grown-up, handicapped daughter was the only other occupant of their small farmhouse. Italian prisoners of war worked their farm.

Huge trees covered the path leading to the farmhouse, making it dark, a little scary. A round, red-faced woman with wispy hair opened the door before Mummy knocked.

"Come on in," she greeted, "nice to meet you. Sit in here and I'll brew some tea."

We walked straight to the kitchen and sat at chairs around the table. I breathed in the warm smell of fresh baked bread. A round loaf decorated a wooden board in the center of the flowery tablecloth. Two jars of jam stood open beside it.

"Would you like some bread and plum jam, dear?" Johnny's foster mother asked me. Plum jam! I looked up at her, mouth salivating. She smiled and told us the plums came off her trees.

"You can call me Aunty Brown if you like, and 'im" – she indicated the farmer with her elbow – "Uncle Tom."

"You won't find any of that imitation raspberry stuff here," she said to Mummy. "Imagine putting sawdust in a jar and selling it! Johnny!" she called through the window over the sink, "your mum's here, come on in now. Just look at 'im."

We both stood up and looked through the window, and there ran Johnny, a black dog jumping up at him, three men chasing him, all of them laughing.

"Stay out all day if I let him," she told us. "Messed in his trousers last week. I made him wash them himself."

Mummy seemed horrified at that, but the foster mother told her not to worry, he was only five and those P.O.W.'s really spoiled him. "Lazy lot, these I-ty's. They'd rather play with Johnny than work," she grinned.

"He does seem to be having a lovely time," said Mummy.

"Well, that's more than can be said of his other foster home," the mother said. I listened carefully as they talked about Mrs. Morgan, "terrible woman," Johnny's foster mother said. Seems that Mrs. Morgan had seven evacuees staying with her, plus her own two sons. The boys slept in an upstairs attic, where they were locked in until morning. This was to keep them from getting into mischief with the girls, or so Johnny's foster mother said. "Imagine that! What if there was a fire?" Mother tutted, shook her head, said, "Shocking!" It was a pair of shoes that rescued him from this place it seems. Mummy had sent Johnny a new pair of shoes, which Mrs. Morgan handed to her own son, giving Johnny the boy's wooden-soled shoes. And when Mummy visited him and found out, she asked him to be moved "immediately," which he was. "I was furious," said Mummy. "You know it's almost impossible to buy shoes these days."

"Or anything else," added the foster mother. "She did it for the money, you know, and the ration books too. Black market, I don't wonder."

I watched Johnny, running wild with the dog, playing in the fields. I licked the sweet-sour plum jam off the bread and chewed slowly to make the taste last. Lucky Johnny, I thought.

"Some more, dear?" the foster mother asked, and before I could answer, she had sliced and jammed three more.

The mothers kept talking, mostly about rationing, "dreadful," about the injured soldiers, "terrible," which I ignored, then Mummy talked about her working, "munitions factory," she said. "Is it dangerous?" Aunty Brown asked. "You might go deaf," Mummy laughed, "it's very noisy." Mummy talked about working almost every day, including Sunday. "Got to do my bit," she said. But she did say that most of the workers were women, all in the "same boat," and they had time to chat at tea breaks. That made me happy, Mummy had friends, she wouldn't be lonely.

Johnny wouldn't come in until the farmer brought him, squiggling and laughing under his arm. He scrambled up to the table, slurped a mug of real milk and crammed his mouth so full of cheese he couldn't speak. Mummy asked him the dog's name and if he was being good, but he didn't even look up.

Then: "Why do you speak 'posh'?" he asked. The first words out of his mouth were so rude, I blushed for him and my mother.

"Because she's a lady," I snapped.

"Then why," he asked, "did you give her weeds and not flowers if she's a lady?" pointing to the bouquet on top of Mummy's handbag. I looked at the flowers and saw the wilted daisies, the drooping grass, the now translucent petals of buttercups, and blushed deeper.

Mummy laughed. "How do you know they're weeds?"

"'Cuz," was his answer. "Can I play now?"

"Ask your Mum," his foster mother told him. He squeezed his eyebrows together, trying to look pathetic.

"Go on then. Be a good boy now." Out the door he went, slamming it behind him.

The two mothers smiled at each other, soft knowing smiles.

We rode back to town together and Mummy left again, with her "be a good girl now."

I went into the dull, dead house and up to the sour-smelling room. Tears ran down my face. I was the one who was supposed to live on a farm with a fluffy dog! Why can't I live on that farm with the kind, smiley lady, fresh milk, plum jam, soft bread! Cheese! Why was Johnny so special! Why couldn't my mother *see* the places I lived in? My stomach tightened with anger.

Why didn't I talk to her, ask her to take me home?

When the boy came to find me for tea, I told him to go away.

"What's wrong?

His kindness made me feel more miserable. I turned away from him and sobbed myself to sleep, muddy shoes still on my feet. In the middle of the night, my eyes popped open. I was more awake than in the mornings. Perhaps Mummy didn't care about me at all.

The next time I saw Johnny, he was sitting up in a hospital bed, covered in spots, chicken pox or measles.

"Hello," I said, and stood nervously by his bed watching him try to scratch the spots through white gloves tied to his hands. I was frightened seeing him in hospital, until he started his whining.

"Let me out of this bloody place," he swore, "right now!"

And I thought how strange that they went to so much trouble to bring me here when I had only seen Johnny twice before during our stay, and neither time was particularly enjoyable. It also surprised me they knew who I was and that I had a brother.

And who were "they" anyway?

CHAPTER 17

THE LADY IN BLACK

Eeyore, the old grey Donkey, stood by the side of the stream, and looked at himself in the water.

"Pathetic," he said. "That's what it is. Pathetic."

He turned and walked slowly down the stream for twenty yards, splashed across it, and walked slowly back on the other side. Then he looked at himself in the water.

"As I thought'" he said. "No better from this side. But nobody minds. Nobody cares. Pathetic, that's what it is." A.A. Milne

The air was hot and still, like before a storm. I pushed on the chipped-paint door, and as it squeaked open, I saw the mother waiting in the passage.

"Come in 'ere, Joan," she said, and opened the door to the living room. She had never used my name before. Her face was extra serious. A "what for" was coming. My legs began to shake, and my stomach tightened. Had my face turned insolent? We went inside the dark, dusty room and she pulled a letter from her apron pocket.

"Your uncle died, in 'ospital," she said. "Is it the one in the Navy?"

I had an uncle? In the Navy? Not in Canada?

My foster mother asked again, "Is it your mother's brother, the one in the Royal Navy?"

My mother had a brother? My face flushed. She was getting impatient, so I said, "Yes." After all, I was seven and should know these things. I also knew I was supposed to cry. That's what she seemed to expect. Why else would she hover around and give me so much attention? But I couldn't cry. It wasn't the same as when I lost Ted or when the old rooster died; all I felt now was curiosity at having an uncle and his dying. I had been told I had an uncle and that he was dead – all this before I ever met him or knew I had one in the Navy. What was the point to that? And, if I had one, perhaps there were more.

Every day I heard about people who died from the war, on the radio, gossip on the street, children in school, the boy's parents, and I was surprised to learn people died of other things.   People died no matter what, birds sang no matter what, the sky did not break. There was another world besides the one of war, the one where the gypsies lived.

Now it was my turn to sit alone in the dusty, musty living room, mourning the dead. That's when I learned to tell time.

There was a fly, trapped behind the glass face of the old clock that stood on the dusty mantlepiece. I looked at the face of the clock with the fly buzzing around, and as I thought about ways to release him from his prison, I noticed the numbers and the hands. The clock was broken, the hands moved in jerky fits and starts – one short and one long. Suddenly, the numbers and hands made sense. I imagined the clock divided into quarters and halves, like a slice of bread. "Quarter to two," "Half past three," and felt very grateful to this fly for his gift of time, and wanted to repay his kindness.

My day for mourning was a muggy one, and after I deciphered the mystery of time, I became fidgety and bored with the waiting. While I was told to sit in this chair, the door was closed and maybe nobody would notice if I moved. So, I climbed up on the fender, opened the door to the clock and released the fly, then looked around for something to do. There was a sewing box on a table by the unused fireplace, which I opened and discovered some reels of cotton and pins in a pincushion shaped like a tomato. I'd knit this fly a scarf, a white one, I decided and set to it. Using two straight pins and some cotton thread, I began my project, copying what I had seen the mother doing. My sweaty fingers slid on the pins, the cotton became grey and, while I didn't want to, I finally gave up.

This room would be better named the "dying" room, I thought as I waited for my turn to be released.

★ ★ ★

It was warm in the garden. I sat in a small wicker chair, felt the sun touch my skin, smelled the sweet grass, listened to the bees hum and the birds call to each other as the feet of my chair slowly sank into the black asphalt. I was home from school, getting over chicken pox or measles caught from my brother I suspected when "they" took me to see him in hospital.

"This 'ere's yer grandmother," said the foster mother. "I'll make a cuppa," she said, and went back into the house.

I turned and looked up. Grandmother. What a lovely word. I was so surprised I had a visitor that I didn't remember my bluebird birthday card and stared at the stranger. Silver curls poked out from under her black straw hat; in fact, she was dressed in black from head to toe. Blue eyes like my mother's peered at me, squinting a little from the sun.

"Hello, Joanie," she said, which told me right away that she knew me. Everyone else called me Joan, if they called me anything at all.

Grandmother walked towards me, I sat, staring at her, wondering what I should do. Then she handed me a lovely doll with cloth molded like skin over her face and body. A girl doll, not a baby doll, wearing clothes I wished were big enough for me: a navy-blue coat and a straw hat with ribbons and silk flowers around the brim, white stockings and black glossy shoes.

"Is she mine?" I asked.

"Yes, dear. I bought her for you. She's French," Grandmother said, then handed me a brown paper bag. "I made these for her." Emptying the bag onto my lap, flowery dresses and petticoats soon covered my grey skirt.

"Oh, she's beautiful," I exclaimed, turning her around, peeking under her skirt; she wore knickers! I gave her a name right away, Shirley.

I changed Shirley's dress and chose a different hat, pretending I had ones to match. I became so absorbed with the beautiful doll I forgot Grandmother was there. Sounds of stifled sobs distracted me, and looking up, I saw her walking away, down the garden path, dabbing her eyes with a hankie.

"Don't yer want yer cuppa?" the mother asked, cup and saucer in hand.

I couldn't hear Grandmother's words but saw the mother's face turn red, and heard her say, "Well, I never!"

And Grandmother was gone.

I knew something special had taken place, as if I had lost something and should be sad. But I felt nothing, except concern for the lady in black, and wondered why she was crying.

I kept Shirley in the bedroom. I didn't want her in the dirty kitchen. I dressed her and talked with her, like she was a real friend and cuddled her at night.

★　★　★

"Look at that 'air. Come 'ere you," the mother said, and tried to pull a comb through the tangled mess. It broke in two.

"C'mon," she said, and putting on her best hat, the one with a feather in the band, walked me out of the door and into town.

We arrived at a barbershop with high steps leading up to the shiny glass door. Gold letters poked out between the criss-crossed tape. It was a very impressive shop, and I felt special.

"Sit there," a tall, fat man said. He wore an apron and looked like a butcher. I sat in a huge, brown leather chair in front of a looking glass, which covered one wall of the room. It was the first time I'd seen myself, except in windows, but then it was only seconds of still between the fiery night skies. I stared in horror at the small, skinny girl with the matted hair who stared back at me, with her dirty skirt and jumper stiff from the need of washing. I had thought I was pretty, like Patsy, but the face that looked at me was pale and hollow, with dark half circles under puffy eyes, and wire-framed glasses hanging off her nose. I was ugly and knew that's why nobody wanted to be my friend.

As if to confirm these thoughts, the barber walked towards me, then took a step back, his face red and angry.

"Get out of here," he yelled. "Filthy, dirty, evacuees!" I stood up, staring, confused, shocked. The mother grabbed my wrist as he kept yelling.

"You should be ashamed of yourself. She's filthy! Crawling alive." He shook a towel at me, as if shooing a cat.

"Well, it ain't my fault. I didn't ask for 'er, did I," sniffed the mother, as she pushed me out of the shop.

"Why wouldn't he cut my hair?"

"Shut up and stop askin' questions," was her angry response. "Now I'll have to wash the sheet!" We walked home in record time. I had to skip to keep up.

At school the next day, I was sent to The Clinic and had my head scrubbed with some awful, stinging, smelly stuff, which would make anything go away. I stood in a puddle of water, trying hard to do what I was told and "keep still!" I tried but still got soaking wet.

Once home, my foster mother cut my hair outside in the garden with her big, old shears. She chopped very quickly, as if she were killing a bush. I kept my hands on my ears to make sure they stayed where they were.

"There, that's better," she said. I ran my hand over my head and felt the bristles where she had chopped too much and long bits that poked out.

The Saturday after my head was scrubbed, the mother announced: "Bath day."

"Don't anyone come in 'ere till I says so." She stoked up the kitchen fire for pots and kettles and slammed the kitchen door shut. I sat on the stairs and listened to her sighs, the clang of metal on metal and the sound of a waterfall splashing into a hollow pool.

It was my turn. I went in after the daughter. The mother was first. The small, round, rusty washtub sat in front of the now dead kitchen fire, filled up halfway. Soggy newspapers lay around it, soaking up spills. I put my clothes on a chair and stood shivering in the cold room, looked in horror at the layer of grey scum floating on top of the water, a mixture of scrubbed off dead skin and soapy film. I made a big circle with my hand, forcing the nasty bits to the side, gingerly stepped into the cold water, rubbed a sliver of soap all over me. There was dirt embedded in the cracks, too deep to go away even though I used enough to make bubbles. The tub was small, and I wondered how the grown-ups fit, unless they didn't mind using the scummy sides which I wanted no part of. I jumped out and dried myself damp with the worn, wet towel.

"Ain't doing that again in an 'urry," the mother said, as she dragged the tub out into the garden to empty. Then she collapsed, panting in a kitchen chair, begging for "a cuppa."

The next day, the mother told me I wasn't going to school that day – "Yer going in 'ospital," she said, and I was to wait by the door for the billeting lady. "It's them warts of yours," she added as a way of explanation. So I waited for the bang on the door. Visions of pointed scissors and bowls of blood filled my thoughts and I planned on how I would bite and kick and yell and run away when the nurse came at me. Run as fast and far as I could.

We didn't go to the clinic, instead we arrived at a building of sorts, that looked like a giant Anderson shelter. Sandbags were stacked outside the doors up to the top. I wondered why.

Inside, it was very busy with nurses walking quickly, their white shoes making squeaky sounds on the polished floor. The billeting lady handed me over to a nurse, who told me to "come along now." And I followed her into a large room with beds along each wall, filled with children. Some were lying down, some sitting up. The sitting up ones mostly had bandages wrapping part of them, their arms or legs or heads. They looked at me. They saw me.

I was led to a bed at the end of a row, and the nurse gave me a nightie and told me to put it on and get into bed, which I did. And then she left. With no grown-ups around, the children started to talk – to me! They wanted to know what was wrong, why was I in hospital, was it my tonsils, my appendix? I had no idea what an appendix was and was so ashamed to tell them I was there for my warts that I said nothing at all.

The smell of hot food wafted into the ward, followed by a trolley wheeled in by a lady dressed in blue. Trays were delivered to the children, and I eagerly waited for mine, which never came. "Nothing by mouth," the lady said. "Sorry, dearie." And that was that.

I needed the toilet – but I had been told to stay in bed, besides, I didn't know where the toilet was anyway. With all the excitement of the day, I fell asleep, only to wake up in a wet bed. Fear, cold and penetrating swept over me. I had wet this clean bed. I was a dirty evacuee. I'd get a "what for" in the morning, I just knew it. And I wasn't even sick, I just had ugly warts on my left hand, nothing important like tonsils or appendix, just ugly, dirty warts.

The bed was dry in the morning, what a relief! But the yellow stain was there as evidence of my sin. There was no "what for," just a click and a slight shake of the head from the nurse before she wheeled me from the ward through a set of doors into a small, brightly lit room.

My body forgot to breathe, my eyes darted around the room, fixing on two men in white coats standing either side of me. Fear filled every pore of my being.

"Well, who to do we have," said one. "Not to worry, dear," said the other. "I'm Doctor Tom, and my friend here is Doctor Peter. We're going to fix you up, good as new," and with those kind words from those kind, smiley faces, I breathed in the air from the mask over my face.

★　★　★

Sounds of laughter greeted me when I came home from school. It was Patsy. There she was with my mother, sitting at the kitchen table. I stood and stared at them both.

"How's my little sister?"

I couldn't answer. I could hardly believe what I saw. She looked all grown-up with wonderful curly hair, thick and shiny, pink lipstick and a pretty dress. She made the dull kitchen come alive.

I smoothed my hair with both my hands, and a little spit, and wiped the skinny worms of dirt on my palms against my skirt.

I wanted to talk to Patsy, like before, tell her how I missed her, but felt awkward and shy and just stared. There were no hugs, and while I longed to be hugged, it was a relief. I didn't want to get Patsy dirty. Patsy smiled at me. I stared some more. "Your tooth," I cried, "it grew back!"

"Silly sausage," she said, and using her tongue, she wiggled the tooth up and down.

"Come here, Joanie," said Mummy, and patted the chair between her and Patsy. We sat with the windows open, drinking tea from chipped cups. A gentle breeze twirled the old net curtains. I felt its soft touch on my skin. The foster mother sat with us too, ladling her precious strawberry jam onto thick slices of bread, slopping some on the table in her display of generosity.

"Yes, train tickets are still allotted out. It's very difficult to travel," Mummy said when the foster mother asked. They were stopping by, "just for a minute," before going to see Johnny and his foster family.

"Patsy's back home now. She hasn't seen Johnny in ages."

"'Ow nice," the mother said.

129

"I thought we'd visit as a special treat, before she starts looking for a job."

"Oh, she were away then?"

"Yes," said Mother, "up North near her father."

I sat there while the words "near her father" buzzed in my head.

"Why? Why did you take Patsy away? Why was I left behind?" That's what I wanted to scream. But I didn't. I wasn't supposed to know. I pretended I hadn't heard.

The voices droned on, interrupted only by a squeak from Patsy when her sticky jam elbow attracted the sting of a bee. She laughed when the foster mother jumped up and beat the table with the corner of her apron. "It doesn't hurt," she said. Patsy was always brave.

Then they left. I stood in front of the closed door for a long time. Mummy didn't kiss me goodbye, but Patsy didn't either.

I forgot to show them Shirley.

CHAPTER 18

THE MORRISON SHELTER

A little Consideration, a little Thought for Others, makes all the difference. A.A. Milne

Except for my mother's two visits, nobody ever came to this house, so it was a surprise when I heard a heavy "bang-bang" on the front door. Wiping her hands on her apron, the mother shuffled from the kitchen in her worn carpet slippers, grumbled under her breath and jerked open the door.

"Wha' yer want?" she said.

I sat on the stairs, watching. An old man stood there in a warden's uniform, his metal hat shading his ruddy face. Behind him, a billeting lady stood, a large, flat bag at her side. I could tell by the way she was dressed with everything matching: a brown woolen suit, a brimmed hat with golden feathers under the band, thick dark-brown stockings and the always big laced-up shoes – more clothes than anyone, except a nun.

"Just checking your shelter situation," said the warden.

"We ain't got one, if that's wot yer mean," responded the mother with a sniff. The old man mumbled away about just doing his job, and don't take it out on him.

"Oh," interrupted the mother when she saw the suited lady.

"Let's go inside shall we," said the billeting lady, and pushed her way into the house.

I scurried downstairs and stood against the passage wall, listened to their footsteps, pacing, biting my nails, wondering if I were going to be moved again.

"Just won't do, you know. Won't do at all." The woman's voice was stern, bossy. They were upstairs, in my bedroom. "Fancy, a big boy like him with that child. Goodness knows what mischief he's thinking. Or what you were thinking for that matter."

"Ain't my fault we ain't got beds," moaned the foster mother.

"What if something happened?"

The stairs shook under the billeting lady's brown shoes. Her angry whispers, "ignorant, backward people," followed as she left the house, leaving the foster mother to close the door. They had been talking about the bed. I wondered how she knew we shared. I stayed away from the mother in case she thought I'd tattled.

Within a few days, a new black metal bed arrived and was placed along the wall in front of the never used fireplace. I was given the new bed. The boy gave me the blanket and the pillow. I missed feeling him near me, and I couldn't hear him breathe now. I cuddled Shirley extra tight.

"I don't like the dark," I told him that night.

"I'll let the moon in, then," he said, and opened the curtains so I could see the sky. It was a full moon, and I watched the shadows of clouds pass in front of it. Shapes of light danced in our room, the bars of my bed reached away from me, the criss-cross tape on the window looked like a lattice rose trellis. I felt the moonbeams touch me, like a cool sun, and floated to sleep in the light of the moon.

★ ★ ★

A black metal box was delivered the day after, in pieces, and assembled inside the house. It was an indoor air-raid shelter, a Morrison shelter.

The shelter was placed in the center of the already overcrowded, dusty living room, which until then was used mostly for storing things and mourning the dead.

"Eh, watch me things," said the mother to the workmen, "ain't no more where them come from."

She watched their every move, hands on hips, tutting, sighing, while they hammered away and groaned under the weight of the metal. The shelter was as high as a table, with a solid top and bottom and thick iron meshing on four sides, with a narrow opening in front. A lumpy grey-striped mattress covered the entire inside.

"Don't know 'ow we'll fit in that," complained the mother.

"It's the biggest we 'ave, missus," said the man, holding a pen and paper for her to sign.

"Forget about a cuppa," she said as she opened the front door and slammed it after them.

The box looked like a coffin.

"Do we have to sleep in there?" I asked the boy that night.

"Just when the raids are bad. If the house gets bombed, all the bricks will fall on top of the shelter, and we won't be crushed," he said. I wanted to take the question back. His parents probably didn't have a Morrison shelter, that's why they died.

Crushing wasn't what scared me though – I was scared of being burned alive. I had nightmares about burning to death since smelling the wet smoke. They would start where I was already swallowed up in sharp, pointed flames – smokeless – shooting upwards from my body. My clothes and hair fly away from me in the scarlet blaze, like wisps of paper released from a fire, and when I look at my arms and legs, I can see white bones poking out from melting flesh. I must keep running to get away from the fire that was eating me – though I could never run fast enough. When I awoke from these fire dreams, I was too frightened to go back to sleep and kept my eyes wide open – just in case.

So I knew what it was like to be burned alive and knew it was far worse than being squashed to death by bricks like the boy's parents or even suffocated like the poor old rooster. And metal gets very hot – just think of a kettle! So how would we get out if the house were on fire?

Every night, for the next two weeks or so, the air raids sounded, and we piled into that moldy, smelly, black box. I thought the whole idea a bad one from the start – and even more so when three adults and two children (one the size of a grown-up) tried to fit inside the small space. We crawled in on hands and knees. I was last, warned with a "don't bring that doll in 'ere!"

The big four lay side by side; my space was across the bottom, blocking the narrow entrance. I had everyone's feet in my face; the smell was sickening. You weren't allowed to move around either, not that there was room for that anyway. "No fidgeting" was the order in the Morrison shelter.

The daughter lay on the outside edge, near my head. I still thought she could be a witch. I turned my face away from her feet, though she was the only one who didn't kick me.

I lay there, rigid, arms clenched at my side, holding my breath between gasps for air. Eyes glued to the top of the shelter, I stared as it moved down, ready to squash us all flat. It was a trap!

The planes droned overhead. I imagined our cage vibrating from the sounds of the engines, or was it the father's snoring? I wanted to scream – but knew I mustn't. I wasn't able to bite my nails either, not enough space to move my arms, and Shirley was not there to cuddle.

Can't sleep, must be ready to run!

When the air raids eased up, we no longer used the Morrison shelter. Perhaps the grown-ups did, which was all right with me. It was always much better watching the sky than hiding in the dark.

★　★　★

The boy had a chart showing pictures of airplanes. He said a warden had given it to him and told him to be on the lookout. He spread the chart out on the floor, and when the planes flew in front of us, we tried to name them.

"There's a Wellington Bomber, see? Only two engines and extra wide wings."

We searched for the American B-17 Flying Fortress. It had four engines and two turrets and flew the fastest of all the bombers, that's what the boy said, though I don't remember spotting one, which was disappointing – it had a great name. Soon I could tell from the sound of the engines "ours" and "theirs," bombers or fighters, and whether they were coming or going. They were quieter when they came back. "They're lighter," the boy explained.

Sometimes, searchlights spoiled our night watch. They lightened the sky in straight moving beams of light, crossing over each other, bleaching out the intensity of the stars in the sky and the gunfire from the airplanes and guns on the ground.

"I wish they'd turn the lights off," I grumbled. The boy laughed.

★　★　★

Walking along the street, kicking a shiny pebble, I heard a loud buzzing, whistling sound, like a giant bee screaming. It began to cough. I looked up at the sky. Clouds floated overhead, just clouds in a blue-grey sky. Then I heard it, a bomb exploding. I put my hands over my head, crouched down, made myself small. The air-raid warning started to scream. I felt a fear so deep, it took away my hunger, it took away my thoughts…my prayers.

The V-1 rocket bombs had come.

Nobody knew what they were at first. One day, they just came low, out of the sky. The rockets came during the day as well as at night. Our familiar world of warnings and night shows changed.

The boy called them "doodlebugs," which made them sound silly and not dangerous – but they were. Now, you did not get to hear the planes flying overhead first, just the sound, the terrible buzzing sound of the rockets.

And I'd wait, huddled up, holding my breath, listening for the noise to stop. The boy told me to count, so I'd know if it was going to drop on us.

"Thousand and one, thousand and two, if we get past one thousand and three, we're all right." So I held my breath and counted, but there was no relief at "one thousand and three," just the sound of the explosion or the silence of the duds.

Months went by, then the doodlebugs were followed by another rocket, the V-2. This time, there was no sound at all, until it hit the ground. I kept my eyes on the sky, shoulders raised to my ears, waiting to see the flash of the rocket. I pictured them landing, exploding into flames. I closed my eyes hard, willing my mind to go blank, say my prayers, hide. When the hollow moan of the all-clear sounded, it felt like it was coming from deep inside of me.

I had become used to the air-raid warnings and all-clears and addicted to the watching. There was a reassurance in the pattern of beginning and end, like a game with rules. With the rockets, the rules were gone, the enemy invisible. I was edgy, nervous, jumping at a leaf falling in front of me, a fly buzzing by the corner of my eye.

The rockets created a new panic, unvoiced, but filling the air with fear. Fear that was contagious. Like thick fogs that chilled me through to my very bones, fear seeped into every cell of my body.

"I don't like these doodlebugs," I told the boy.

"Not to worry, Joan. The planes will shoot them down. Most of them that get this far are duds, anyway," he told me. He always said the right thing to make me feel brave.

The father didn't turn on the radio now. They didn't talk about the rockets at all. They were quiet, sipping tea, rolling cigarettes from tobacco scraped from butts off the street, knitting scarves they never finished. I wondered if everyone had silently agreed that by not talking about rockets, they could pretend nothing happened and they would go away. Just like the bombed house with the smoking bricks, and the old rooster, the old hen.

I thought about the whispered things I overheard: the people who were crushed or burned to death, soldiers stranded on beaches, the thousands of bombs dropped by "ours" that destroyed a beautiful city, the number of dead pilots whom I felt I knew, and my mother – though I couldn't remember what she looked like anymore, only the sound of her voice and the smell of roses that surrounded her.

Best to keep away from sad thoughts, they had a way of increasing in speed as they spiraled downwards to a deep dark place. Think about fat red robins, friendly horses, the pictures Patsy had taken me to see. Think about the sky that goes on forever without breaking. Think about Ted. I'd almost forgotten about Ted. He had left me such a long time ago now, though I still loved him.

Remember, "Jesus loves you."

★ ★ ★

The boy came to find me, I was sitting in the garden, rubbing knives up and down in the black earth, "cleaning them," just like the mother told me. Didn't make a bit of sense to me, but there was nothing else going on that day, and nothing really made sense anyway.

"Want to see something special?" he asked. I wanted to see anything at all, so I stood up and he took me by the hand, finger to lips, and led me out of the garden onto the street and around the corner towards town.

People stood on the pavements, wardens stood in front of them, stopping them from crossing the streets, and along came army trucks and guns on wheels and soldiers marching, like in a parade. The sound of the trucks and the tanks and the boots vibrated inside of me, and I wanted to run alongside them, be a part of all this excitement.

"Come on," the boy said, grabbed my arm, and off we set, "to the railway." We ran and stood on the embankment where the train tracks passed. Trains went by, they always did of course, but these were special, filled with more soldiers and more guns and trucks, and we cheered them on, and made V signs with our fingers.

"Something important is going on," he said.

Well of course it was. Today was the most exciting, wonderful day ever, so it had to be important.

"Maybe the war's over," I said.

"Maybe," he agreed.

But I really didn't care. It was enough to be here with the boy and be part of something amazing.

CHAPTER 19

FAREWELL

Promise me you'll never forget me, because if I thought you would
I'd never leave. A.A. Milne

One winter day, long before spring came, the boy left as if he were going to school, except he never came back. He didn't say goodbye to me. I just didn't see him when I came home from school. I waited for the mother or father to say something, and when they didn't, I thought something bad had happened, that maybe he had been killed by a rocket. Maybe he was fifteen and had to leave because there would be no more government allowance for the mother. Perhaps he joined the army. Maybe he ran away. I was too frightened of the answer to ask.

In bed, I fretted, wondering where he might be. I knew he wouldn't be at his own home. He had no home. The room seemed larger, felt colder, darker. I looked but could not even see his shadow. He had left nothing behind, as if he hadn't been there, as if he had been only an imaginary friend.

After school, I sat on the stairs until it was bedtime and waited for him. And then I pretended he would arrive another day. Just walk in the door, smile, say, "hello."

I wished I knew his name. I didn't want to miss him. I bit my lip to keep from crying.

Since his parents died, he had worked for money after school: running errands for neighbors, sweeping out the grocers, hunting for coal and twigs, all of which he gave the mother. So while we had seen less of each other that year, I had known that at night he would always be in our shared room, making me feel brave. Whether I wanted it or not, he had become my friend, my only friend. Now he was gone, and I never thanked him. Didn't say goodbye.

I listened to the night noises, like the boy had told me. "Hear that?" he would ask, "heavy and slow, listen," and he made a droning sound like the engines, a circular sound, loud then soft, loud then soft, "that's a bomber and he's going, when he comes back, he won't sound so loud."

The first night the air-raid sirens screamed, cold fear stopped my breath and I scrambled under our old bed, and as I crawled on the dusty floor among the giant fluff balls, I saw his airplane chart. I knew he had left it there for me. He didn't want me hiding under the bed. I clutched it tight, crawled back out to our place in front of the window and knelt there as if he were still with me.

We had talked about the fighter planes, the Hurricanes and the Spitfires, which we both admired, and the P52 Mustang, named after wild horses. My favourite was the graceful Spitfire, much slimmer than the Hurricane, and faster than the wind. I truly loved the brave Spitfire, alone in the sky, protecting us. Such a small plane – so quick, so clever.

"Look at him, look at him," the boy would whisper, and I'd follow his pointing finger to the solid shape of the sleek fighter flying in the unbroken sky.

I remembered when he told me the sky would never break. I had found comfort in that, though it still didn't make sense. Everything I saw, everything I knew, had a beginning and an end. It must be true, because he said so. But I wondered how the sky could go on forever and ever without ending, and then wondered what would be behind the end if indeed it did have an ending, and if it did have an ending, wouldn't that be a beginning?

Every night I thought about air raids, how the lights and noises flashed and bounced, like thunder and lightning, just a little bit separate from each other. They were my connection to my friend, the boy. They kept me company in the sour-smelling room, in the house where nobody spoke my name.

* * *

Shortly after the boy left, two children arrived from London, about my age, dirty faces with snot running in black lines from noses to lips, and hair standing stiffly in all directions. They were part of the new evacuees, escaping the rocket bombs.

Their clothes were baggy and dirty, dirtier even than mine, the children happy and noisy, and spoke in a way that sounded like a foreign English language, though I knew the swear words that counted for every other. I was told to wait outside in the garden, so I stood and looked in through the open window. They sang a song and all the grown-ups laughed. I hoped the children would stay. But soon, *they* showed up again and took them away. These children were not wanted here.

That was the first time I heard singing in this house, there was little laughter too, so I thought I would sing the song that had made everyone laugh and make my foster family happy. I stood in front of the kitchen table, hands behind my back, and performed. I must have sung it badly, before I could finish the mother walloped me on the side of my head so hard my ears rang.

"Wot would yer mum think?" she yelled.

* * *

Days go by, one after the other, each one indistinguishable from the last, and I wait and try not to think about what I wait for. I make up new stories of my family in my world of make believe. This world is mine and mine alone to create, to control, and that's where I live with my mother and roses, away from the dead house and sour smells...the rocket bombs.

CHAPTER 20

VICTORY IN EUROPE

*You can't stay in your corner of the Forest waiting for others to come
to you. You have to go to them sometimes.* A.A. Milne

8 May 1945

S un shone through the window, turning my closed eyelids pink. Spring
is here again at last. I jumped out of bed, ready to hunt for daffodils,
crocus. I opened my door and, for the first time ever, heard voices, loud
and excited, coming from the kitchen. The boy was back! I ran fast down
the stairs and stood in the open doorway. He wasn't there. But the mother,
father and daughter were, the three of them, talking at once, even the
daughter was making noises! I stood, open-mouthed.

"It's over," the father said. He turned up the radio, louder. I stood frozen
in place.

Cheers filled the room, and the radio announcer described the scene
from Trafalgar Square, where "over a million people have gathered in cel-
ebration." The war in Europe has ended.

What did that mean? What should I do? Where would I go?

I sat on the earthen floor in the old garden shed and felt I had just
arrived. The beetles scurried around, busy as ever, but I didn't feel like

playing. The BBC said it was 1945. I must be nine years old. I hadn't thought of it before – there were no birthday cards, no markers – but now I was nine, almost grown-up.

I walked around in a daze. Days or weeks passed. There was no school. I was in a suspended state, out of time and not connected to anywhere. I heard the birds sing but didn't recognise their song. I walked in the garden, with the fluffy carrot tops and green vines waiting for their peas and beans; it looked forlorn, neglected. And all the while, the mother rushed around, sweeping, dusting, pulling and scraping tape off windows, handing it to her daughter who wrapped it around her arms, laughing. I watched them play. I didn't know they could laugh, play.

I sat on my bed with Shirley. Except for being in need of a wash, she looked beautiful, and I hugged her close.

★   ★   ★

"Cum 'ere," the mother said, "I got yer a present." She tied a crushed blue ribbon in my cropped hair – the first time I had a ribbon in my hair since my fourth birthday – and scrubbed my face for me.

"There yer are, good as new," she said. "Put on this 'er dress, 'urry up now, yer leaving." She handed me a dress. My very first dress.

"Am I going to another foster home?" I asked.

"Yer goin' 'ome."

Going home? How? I went to my room and put on the dress. My hands shook. The hem was crooked and bulky from being rolled up and short-ened, the shoulders hung halfway down my arms, but it was almost new, and clean. I looked at the boy's empty bed, the tattered curtains, the stained wallpaper. This had been my world, my safe place, this sour-smelling room.

Goosebumps crept up and down my body. I picked up Shirley and wrapped her clothes in my old jumper. I placed the airplane chart on his bed, just in case the boy came back, and closed the door for the last time.

"'Ere, yer still need these," the mother said, and handed me my two ration books and a bundle of clothes, wrapped in newspaper, tied with a piece of precious string. I picked up my gas mask.

"Yer won't need tha' there no more," the father said.

Holding Shirley under my arm, I clutched the mask to me with both hands. You weren't supposed to go anywhere without it!

"Now, now, let it go," he said, and wrenched the cardboard box from me. I felt naked, empty. That mask had been part of my life, a burden at first, then a companion. I stared at his face, seeing it for the first time; it was a kind face, whiskery, weathered, and kind.

"Tha'll be 'er," said the mother, going to answer the rat-tat-tat on the door.

"Hello, Joanie," said Patsy. "Let's go home," she smiled and took hold of my hand, tight. I stared up at her. Her hair was full and curly, down to her shoulders, she wore lipstick and a flowery dress with a blue jacket. She looked beautiful and bright and clean. I turned away from my foster mother. I turned away from them all. I didn't say "goodbye" to this family who had sheltered me.

That was the last time I remember seeing them. They remain in my memory as they did in life, nameless, shapeless, faded figures.

★ ★ ★

As in my dreams, when I magically float from place to place, there I was, climbing off the bus at the railroad station with my big sister Patsy holding my hand. I felt her soft fingers wrapped around mine, grounding me. I became aware of the noisy children, the cool air brushing my face, the dirt in the creases of my wrists, the lines of white where sweat trickled down my arms.

Huffing and clanging, a train made its entrance along the tracks and sighed as it stopped in front of us. We climbed the steps and boarded the crowded train. Patsy slammed the heavy door shut behind us. I heard the loud bang. It was so final, like an ending. I was leaving the town where I had spent more than half my childhood.

I gave it not a backward glance, not a thought about it or the people who lived there. I held Patsy's hand and clutched Shirley tight to my chest. They were real, everything else a bad dream.

★ ★ ★

What's wrong with the train? It's taking too long to start. Maybe it's broken... It could be the wrong train. I heard a sound. An air-raid siren. I cringed, ready to run. It wasn't over. I knew it would come back. I heard it again. A whistle, the signal for our train to leave.

The conductor waved his green flag, and the train, with jerky starts, clanged and strained slowly out of the single platform station.

Everyone pushed and shoved for a place by an open window in the carriage door or corridor. Free at last, we all yearned to hang out the windows, look ahead, watch the smoke coming in black streams from the train engine, feel the cool wind outside, even if only on an outstretched hand.

Being one of the few grown-ups, Patsy was able to move through the crowd to a prime spot by an open window in the corridor of the packed train. I leaned out and felt the wind play with my stiff hair. I took a deep breath and exhaled with a long sigh.

"Won't need these," said Patsy, and flung my wrapped rags out the window. "I'll give you some of mine." Pretty, clean clothes! I closed my eyes so Patsy couldn't see my tears.

★   ★   ★

We stopped several times on the way to London, each time, more children squeezed on board. At one stop, American soldiers leaned out of windows on a train across from ours. "Got any gum, chum?" reverberated across the track.

The soldiers, all smiles, aimed sweets and chewing gum and fruit at our outstretched hands. (Their teeth are so white!) Patsy caught an orange – I couldn't believe it, and nobody could take it from her – it was wrapped around her thumb. And there it was, like a prize, held up high from the grabbing hands, in all its juicy glory.

As Patsy peeled the skin away, I watched the neat orange sections appear and drooled. I remembered the picture at Mrs. Croft's and the luscious orange held in the soldier's hand. Now I'd know what a real orange tasted like.

★   ★   ★

Houses abruptly replaced trees and fields, their back gardens ending where the tracks began. I had counted the stations and at six, Patsy said it was our stop. She opened the train door.

Legs shaking under me, I climbed down steep steps, jumped over the wide deep gap to the platform.

My mother was waiting. She was there. A flowery blue scarf draped around her neck and waved around the collar of her dark-blue jacket. I hadn't dared think she would be waiting for me, and there she was, my pretty Mummy. I looked at the dirt on my arms, my knees. I walked towards her.

My knees wobbled, my legs walked slowly. What did I say? My dirty socks had disappeared into my scruffy shoes, my crooked hem… Two years had passed since she last saw me. Would Mummy like me? Want me?

"Hello, Joanie." I'd dreamed of hearing these words and how I would respond, but I stood like a statue, without voice or movement.

Mummy reached for my shaking hand. Her hand was soft, cool, clean in my sticky grip. Curls bounced around her face, pearl earrings swung. I smelled her scent of roses and my own sour smell of unwashed body, hair.

Mummy guided me out of the huge station. I gaped at the world we stepped into. Clutched Shirley tighter under my arm.

Broken windows boarded up, broken buildings falling down, dust, smoke, smells.

Cars and bright-red, double-decker buses vied for space on a wide, busy road, petrol fumes filled the air, dirt swirled in circles, carrying soiled newspapers and leaves up and down and around, horns honked, engines growled, people rushed in all directions, every one of them racing to somewhere else.

I pulled back. Waited for the air-raid warning to scream. I felt my hand, sticky from the juice of the orange, in Mother's soft grip, took a deep breath, braced myself against the lorries that tugged at my skirt, the grit that bit my legs…the noise. I looked up at my mother. She was real, with her red lipstick shining, her pearl earring swinging. I thought of my dreams.

Tonight, Mummy will hug me goodnight. I am going home! Our home will be beautiful, with flowers and curtains and furniture that didn't grow fuzz. I had dreamt about it so often, I could almost see it. We will have hot food, laugh and talk to each other, live without fear of bombs, of fire. The waiting is over.

We walked in silence along St. John's Hill Road, past boarded up buildings and open spaces, walls propped up by wooden beams, like buttresses on a castle. Some of the walls had wallpaper clinging to them. I could tell by the patterns the bedrooms, the kitchens. And the broken buildings mixed with neat little shops: a baker's, a dairy, a butcher's, a knitting shop and Mr. Dollimore's newspaper shop mixed with big white houses, pubs, churches…rubble, holes.

Every crack in a wall, every bolt in a beam planted itself in my memory, as if my mind was a camera. Mummy kept walking, she didn't seem to notice the buildings, the smells…me.

We turned down a side street.

"Here we are."

My heart stopped, started again. My legs walked, I followed. The corner house was a bomb site, its walls neglected rubble. Concrete air-raid shelters, smelling of urine and disinfectant formed a long row of bleak, grey boxes all the way down the hill to the bottom of the street, where another bomb site sat. There were no trees. Weeds filled the small front gardens. Low brick walls replaced most of the black iron railings.

Was this home, this street with windowless air-raid shelters running the length of it? The place I had dreamt about, waited for – the home that would be more beautiful than the dingy, moldy houses in Chertsey?

My mind turned numb.

CHAPTER 21

HOMECOMING

If the person you are talking to doesn't appear to be listening, be patient. It may simply be that he has a small piece of fluff in his ear. A.A. Milne

We arrived at our house, in the middle of a string of twenty-odd houses in the short, narrow street. Mother let go my hand and opened the gate. Its hinges squeaked. We walked over chipped mosaic tiles, orange, green, white, to the white stone doorstep where a black iron boot scraper waited for mud. Glass panels sparkled in the dark-green door, like eyes, one green etched with a pattern, and one plain white. Why hadn't they smashed when the bombs dropped?

Mother pushed wide the door. A round table with blood-red roses in a crystal vase stood in the hall and wide, carpeted stairs led up to a landing straight ahead, which my mother climbed. The passage continued to another set of closed doors.

Why were we going up the stairs and not along that passageway? Why did we have only half a house? I thought people shared houses only during a war, like the room we had in Brighton.

We climbed in silence to the second floor. The stairs led to the kitchen, which had a glass-topped door looking out onto a wrought-iron balcony with steps leading to the garden. We turned right, past closed doors, climbed another short staircase, with a staircase opposite, and into the living room, which faced the street.

The room was cool and bright and smelled of lavender polish. A wide window faced us, and then a bay window to the left, all with lace panels and flowery curtains letting sunlight into the room. A large, white marble mantlepiece stood against one wall, surrounding an ornate black iron fireplace. Paintings hung on all the walls, except one, where missing wallpaper and clumps of plaster exposed the lath skeleton of the house, behind which dark spaces loomed. I shuddered…turned away. Plaster carvings decorated the high ceiling with Tudor roses and oak leaves, unbroken except for a section over the bay window. I stared at that broken space, wondering if it could be mended.

Where were the cushions I'd lie on in front of the fire? They were pink, soft and silky. Except for the smell of polish and roses in vases, nothing was familiar. This wasn't my house. Something was wrong.

Johnny stood in the middle of the room, picking at a scab on his knee. There he was, in front of me, taller than me and bony. His hair still stuck out in odd directions, and his ears stuck out from the sides of his head. He looked as scruffy as I, with his grey flannel short pants stained with dirt, his crumpled shirt collar poking out from his knitted striped vest, and his knee-high socks sagging around the tops of his scuffed-up shoes.

Patsy walked into the room, and hands at our sides, we formed a circle. No one spoke.

So here we are again, I thought, the four of us, like all those years ago in Brighton. But now I didn't know them, and they didn't know me. We were strangers…and I was the last one to come home.

★ ★ ★

Johnny kept pleading, over and over, louder and louder, until his words finally penetrated my thoughts, "Mum, can I go out now? Please!" He did that pathetic thing with his eyebrows, "My mates can go out. Their mums let them." He dragged out the word "their."

I stared at the carpet, counting the patterns, holding the tears in my throat, longing, waiting, hoping, praying Mummy will hug me, tell me I'm home now, trying not to think, not to feel.

"It's teatime, and Joanie must be hungry," Mother said. "I'll get you all something to eat."

I followed her into the scullery and watched her put the kettle on for tea. She took a loaf of white bread from the bin, and placing it on a wooden board, sliced six thin slices, which she toasted under the grill while she opened a tin of baked beans, emptied them in a saucepan and heated them on the stove.

"I want eggs with my toast," Johnny said. Mother told him we couldn't have chickens in London.

"London stinks," he said, and went out to play without eating, slamming the door behind him. I heard Mummy sigh.

Mummy, Patsy and I, sat at the kitchen table covered in a white cloth with lace in the center and on the edges, with four sharp crease lines made by a hot iron. Bean juice overflowed on my flowery china plate, a golden-brown, sweet-tasting liquid that I licked off my lips so as not to waste a drop. Patsy didn't want to eat, but the three of us drank tea together from cups without chips or cracks, and I tried not to finish the delicious treat too quickly or make a mess on the tablecloth.

Mummy broke the silence, "You must be tired, Joanie. I'll get a bath ready," she said.

She poured a hot bath for me, filled almost to the top. I watched as she shook crystals like unpolished diamonds into the water and saw them dissolve into sweet-smelling steam. Rose-scented soap, talcum powder with a big pink powder puff, "swansdown," she said, and a whole washcloth and a fluffy towel were placed on a stool, not rags, which Mummy said was just for me – and a pink nighty made from soft cotton flannel, Patsy's "one for spare."

My first real bath for as long as I could remember. I inhaled the perfume and the fragrance cleared my head, like the smell of rain when it first falls.

"Here, Joanie, I'll help you bathe," Mother said. To my horror, Mother turned me around and began opening the buttons on my dress. Colour flooded my face! *I cannot have her bathe me. I cannot have her see me naked.* I wrapped my arms around my body, held my dress tight, turned away.

Voice shaking, I said, "Mummy, I'm a big girl now." The words came out, without thinking. Cruel, hurtful words.

Mother's hand dropped from my shoulder, and, lowering her head, she left, closing the door softly behind her.

I wanted to take the words back…thank her…ask her to bathe me, but I couldn't. I was nine-and-a-half years old!

I climbed into the huge tub, hollow, empty, shivering, seeing my mother's sad face. I rubbed the round pink soap slowly in my hair, over my body, between my toes, dried with my fluffy towel and put on the pink nighty, which touched the floor.

My body tingled; I was clean. The years of dirt washed away. I felt the warmth of soft flannel against my skin, the slippers, fuzzy against my feet. The lightness of my body.

I stepped quietly into the living room. Mummy was sitting by the fire in a big, soft chair, reading the paper. "I'm sorry, Mummy. I love you, Mummy," that's what I wanted to say, but I stood still, waiting.

"Come by the fire, Joanie," she said, "I set it to take the chill off. You can dry your hair." Precious coal, I thought, and it's not even winter. Was it for me?

I knelt on the carpet in front of the fire and flipped my hair over my face. It didn't take long to dry. I could feel my scalp, loose, light, my hair silky as I smoothed it flat. I stared into the flames and saw the blue-white ones streaking straight up into the chimney. I looked at my mother, she put down her paper. "Time for bed," she said.

I followed her up the stairs, under a skylight, to the huge room I would share with Patsy and Johnny. Two dressers stood guard on either side of the small fireplace, a dressing table with three looking glasses sat under the open window, a matching wardrobe, its inlaid flowery pattern shining golden in the lamplight, stood against the far wall. A pink satin eiderdown covered my bed, and when Mother pulled it back, I saw lace trim on the white pillowcase. I felt the sheets, smooth from starch, the mattress soft under my body, the pillow, filled with feathers. Mother tucked me in, lifting up the mattress a little as she did so. "There you are, all snug. Sleep tight, Joanie," she said. She switched off the light and closed the door behind her.

Clean and warm, I cuddled Shirley tight, watched the lace curtains move gently at the small bay window, pushed out to let in the soft night air…listened to the safe silence. I was home. The broken plaster didn't matter, the torn wallpaper didn't matter. Nothing mattered. I was home.

I sighed, a deep sigh I felt all the way to my toes. I said my prayers.

I waited, but sleep didn't come. The room seemed darker now. And the longer I stared, the more shapes I saw in the shadows. The shapes began to move. I wriggled and squirmed in fear, but the covers held me tight to the bed, like wrappings on a mummy, squishing my toes flat. My arms wanted to bend, to be free of the covers that held me down. How could I run? How could I hide if I couldn't move? I kicked until my feet were free, pulled the covers loose and placed my arms on the outside. The shadows slowly faded away. My heart stopped beating in my ears. I turned onto my side, wrapped my arms around Shirley, kissed the top of her head and closed my eyes.

There was a squeaking sound, coming from the door! Something was there! Standing in the open doorway…lit up by the skylight behind it! I couldn't see what it was, but it was huge! And coming closer! It had finally found me. I knew it would. I screamed, jumped out of bed, ran to the window, ready to climb out onto the roof. Run away! I screamed, "Go away, go away!"

"Joanie! Joanie. It's only me, silly billy. It's just me. Who did you think it was?" Patsy said, then stretched out her arms to me, spoke softly. "Come on, get back in bed, or what's left of it."

Heart pounding, I stared at her, my big sister. She was here, with me once more. I took a deep breath, let it out, slowly. Thought of the big bully who stole my marbles. Patsy's missing tooth…

Then I turned and looked at my pretty bed. I had made a mess of it alright. Mummy would be cross. I just knew it. It was a beautiful bed, the one of my dreams, and I knew how hard it was to wash sheets and get them dry. The foster mother told me, that's why she stopped giving me one. I must try harder to be good.

Still shaking, I climbed back into bed. *Tomorrow. I'll start tomorrow. I'll tell Mummy all the things I've waited to say: how much I've missed her, how frightened I had been, how alone I had felt. How much I love her. As soon as I get up, I'll tidy the bed. Then everything will be perfect, like in my dreams.*

And there were books in the living room. I saw a bookcase by the side of the fireplace. I cuddled Shirley tighter. "There are books downstairs," I told her. "We can read real books."

I closed my eyes. I fell asleep.

ACKNOWLEDGEMENT

Grateful acknowledgment is made to my dear friend Shan Correa, who helped me through the hard times and whose encouragement and support never faltered. And to Lillian Cunningham who, through her weekly writing retreats, creates a safe place to explore memories.

AUTHORS BIO

Joan Kelleher Gencarelli was born in London, England and has lived in Hawaii since the early sixties, where her two children and various dogs, cats, ducks and fish thrived. Joan's first career was as a technical writer who created operating procedures and systems requirements for the casualty insurance industry.

In 2002, Joan "started writing for fun," which resulted in short stories inspired by ten years as an Ex-pat's wife in Beijing, Seoul and Bangkok. Childhood memories of WWII evacuation were incorporated into a short story, "Evacuation – There and Back" which became part of the BBC WWII People's War archives. Among other stories, one published in the literary journal, *The Rainbird*, was awarded the Golden Plover Award from the Windward Arts Council. In 2006, she received the Lorin Tarr Gill Honorable Mention award for non-fiction.

Joan is an avid traveler and longs to visit the few places on her list that she has not yet seen, take in the sights, meet interesting people, sample the foods on offer, and shop!!!

PHOTO GALLERY

Johnny, age 2, and his floppy-eared dog.

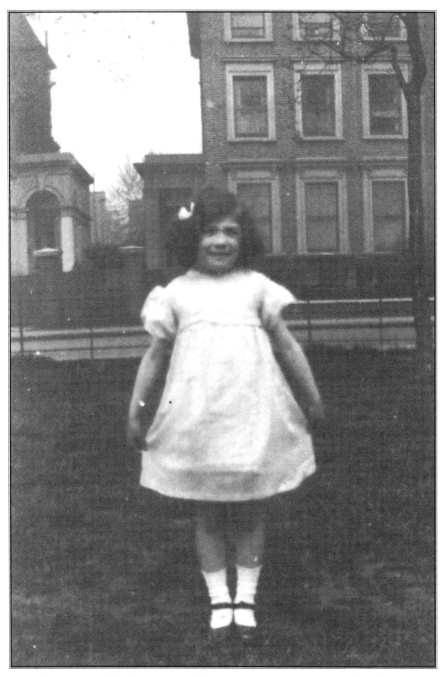

Patsy, age 10, showing off her new summer dress – London,
July 1939. Taken at Spencer Park, a peaceful green space
two streets away from home, on one of our walks.

Joan age 3 – London, August 1939, taken at Battersea Park Playground.

Grandma, The Lady in Black c. 1938

Mother, Mrs. Jupp (the lady who gave us our room at the top of
the stairs), Johnny, Joan, and Ted. Brighton, Spring, 1940

Made in the USA
Middletown, DE
25 March 2023

27669913R00097